Shiukichi Shigemi

**A Japanese boy**

Shiukichi Shigemi

**A Japanese boy**

ISBN/EAN: 9783337168490

Printed in Europe, USA, Canada, Australia, Japan

Cover: Foto ©ninafisch / pixelio.de

More available books at **www.hansebooks.com**

# A JAPANESE BOY

BY HIMSELF

NEW YORK
HENRY HOLT AND COMPANY
1890

*COPYRIGHTED*, 1880,
By SHIUKICHI SHIGEMI.

# CONTENTS.

PAGE

### CHAPTER I.
MY BIRTHPLACE—MY GRANDFATHER—TENJINSAN, 7

### CHAPTER II.
OLD-FASHIONED SCHOOL—MY SCHOOLMASTER—THE SCHOOL-HOUSE, . . . . . . 14

### CHAPTER III.
THE KITCHEN—DINNER—FOOD, . . . . 19

### CHAPTER IV.
GAMES—NEW SCHOOL—IMITATING THE WEST—MORE ABOUT MY SCHOOLMASTER—PUNISHMENTS AT SCHOOL, . . . . . . . . . 25

### CHAPTER V.
BATHS—EVENINGS AT HOME—JAPANESE DANCING AND MUSIC, . . . . . . . . 33

### CHAPTER VI.
AMATEUR ACTORS AND REAL ACTORS AND ACTRESSES—JAPANESE THEATRE, . . . . 45

### CHAPTER VII.
WRESTLING—STORY-TELLERS—PICNIC AND PICNIC GROUNDS—AN OLD CASTLE AND A TRADITION, 57

## CONTENTS.

### CHAPTER VIII.
ANGLING—A PIOUS OLD LADY AND HER ADVENTURES, . . . . . . . . . 67

### CHAPTER IX.
THE YAITO—A WITCH-WOMAN—AUNT OTSUNÉ, MISS CHRYSANTHEMUM AND MR. PROSPERITY, . . 75

### CHAPTER X.
NEW-YEAR'S DAY—THE MOCHI-MAKING—OLD-TIME OBSERVANCES, . . . . . . . 87

### CHAPTER XI.
KITE-FLYING—HOW I MADE MY KITE—MY UNCLE AND HIS BIG KITE—OTHER NEW-YEAR GAMES—HOW WE END OUR NEW-YEAR HOLIDAYS, . 96

### CHAPTER XII.
OTHER JAPANESE HOLIDAYS—TANABATA AND INOKO, THE BOYS' DAYS—THE SHINTOISTIC AND BUDDHISTIC ABLUTION MASS, . . . . 105

### CHAPTER XIII.
OUR PRIEST AND BOY-PRIEST—OUR DOG GEM—SHAKA'S BIRTHDAY, . . . . . . 112

### CHAPTER XIV.
THE FESTIVALS OF LOCAL DEITIES—SCHOOL AGAIN, AND SOME ACCOUNT OF MY SCHOOL-FELLOWS—CONCLUSION, . . . . . . . . 121

# PREFATORY LETTER.

Prof. Henry W. Farnam:

*Dear Sir:*—My motives in writing this jejune little volume are, as you are aware, two:

1st. There seems to be no story told in this country of the Japanese boy's life by a Japanese boy himself. The following rambling sketches are incoherent and extremely meagre, I own; but you must remember that they are a boy's talks. Give him encouragement, and he will tell you more.

2d. The most important of my reasons is my desire to obtain the means to prosecute the studies I have taken up in America. Circumstances have obliged me to make my own way in this hard world. If I knew of a better step I should not have resorted to an indiscreet juvenile publication —a publication, moreover, of my own idle experiences, and in a language the alphabet of which I learned but a few years ago.

To you my sincere acknowledgments are due for encouraging me to write these pages. This kindness is but one of many, of which the public has no knowledge.

I am, sir,
Yours very truly,
SHIUKICHI SHIGEMI.

NEW HAVEN, CT., September, 1889.

# A JAPANESE BOY.

## CHAPTER I.

I was born in a small seaport town called Imabari, which is situated on the western coast of the island of Shikoku, the eastern of the two islands lying south of Hondo. The Imabari harbor is a miserable ditch; at low tide the mouth shows its shallow bottom, and one can wade across. People go there for clam-digging. Two or three little streams empty their waters into the harbor. A few junks and a number of boats are always seen standing in this pool of salt-water. In the houses surrounding it, mostly very old and ramshackle, are sold eatables and provisions, fishes are bought from the boats, or shelter is given to sailors.

When a junk comes in laden with rice, commission merchants get on board and strike for bargains. The capacity of the vessel is measured by the amount of rice it can carry. The grain merchant carries about him a good-sized bamboo a few inches long, one end of which is sharpened and the other closed, being cut just at a joint. He thrusts the pointed end into bags of the rice. The bags are rice-straw, knitted together roughly into the shape of barrels. Having taken out samples in the hollow inside of the bamboo stick, the merchant first examines critically the physical qualities of the grains on the palm of his hand, and then proceeds to chew them in order to see how they taste. Years of practice enable him to state, after such simple tests, precisely what section of the country the article in question came from, although the captain of the vessel may claim to have shipped it from a famous rice-producing province.

About the harbor are coolies waiting for work. They are strong, muscular men, thinly clad, with easy straw sandals on. Putting a little cushion on the left shoulder, a coolie rests the rice-bag upon it and walks away from the ship to a store-house; his left hand passed around the burden and his right holding a short, stout, beak-like, iron hook fastened in the bag. In idle moments the coolies get together and indulge in tests of strength, lifting heavy weights, etc.

At a short distance to the right from the entrance of the harbor is a sanitarium. It is a huge, artificial cave, built of stone and mortar and heated by burning wood-fires in the inside. After it is sufficiently warmed the fire is extinguished, the smoke-escape shut, and the oven is ready for use. Invalids flock in with wet mats, which they use in sitting on the scalding rocky floor of the oven. Lifting the mat that hangs like a curtain at the entrance, they plunge into the suffocating hot air and remain there some time and emerge again into daylight, fairly roasted and smothered. Then they speedily make for the sea and bathe in it. This process of alternate heating and cooling is repeated several times a day. It is to cook out, as it were, diseases from the body. For some constitutions the first breath of the oven immediately after the warming is considered best, for others the mild warmth of later hours is thought more commendable. I, for myself, who have accompanied my mother and gone through the torture, do not like either very much. The health-seekers rent rooms in a few large cottages standing near by. In fact, they live out of town, free from business and domestic cares, pass time at games, or saunter and breathe pure air under pine-trees in the neighborhood. The establishment is opened only during summer time. A person ought to get well in whiling away in free air those glorious summer days without the aid of the roasting scheme.

To the left of the harbor along the shore stands the main body of Imabari. Mt. Myozin heaves in sight long before anything of the town can be seen. It is not remarkable as a mountain, but being so near my town, whenever I have espied it on my return I have felt at home. I can remember its precise outline. As we draw nearer, white-plastered warehouses, the sea-god's shrine jutting out into the water, and the castle stone walls come in our view. You observe no church-steeple, that pointed object so characteristically indicative of a city at a distance in the Christian community. To be sure, the pagoda towers toward the sky in the community of Buddhists; but it is more elaborate and costly a thing than the steeple, and Imabari is too poor to have one.

Facing the town, in the sea, rises a mountainous island; it encloses with the neighboring islets the Imabari sound. A report goes that on this island lies a gigantic stone, apparently immovable by human agency, so situated that a child can rock it with one hand. Also that a monster of a tortoise, centuries old, floats up occasionally from an immeasurable abyss near the island to sun itself; and those who had seen it thought it was an island.

Very picturesque if viewed from the sea but painfully poverty-stricken to the sight when near, is a quarter closely adjoining Imabari on the north. It is on the shore and entirely made up of fishermen's homes. The picturesque, straw-thatched cottages stand under tall, knotty pine-trees and send up thin curls of smoke. Their occupants are, however, untidy, careless, ignorant, dirty; the squalid children let loose everywhere in ragged dress, bareheaded and barefooted. The men, naked all summer and copper-colored, go fishing for days at a time in their boats; the women sell the fishes in the streets of Imabari. A fisher-woman carries her fishes in a large, shallow, wooden tub that rests on her head; she also carries on her breast a babe that cannot be left at home.

Imabari has about a dozen streets. They are narrow, dirty, and have no sidewalks; man and beast walk the same path. As no carriages and wagons rush by, it is perfectly safe for one to saunter along the streets half asleep. The first thing I noticed upon my landing in New York was, that in America a man had to look out every minute for his personal safety. From time to time I was collared by the captain who had charge of me with, "Here, boy!" and I frequently found great truck horses or an express wagon almost upon me. In crossing the streets, horse-cars surprised me more than once in a way I did not like, and the thundering engine on the Manhattan road caused me to crouch involuntarily. Imabari is quite a different place; all is peace and quiet there. In one section of the town blacksmiths reside exclusively, making the street black with coal dust. In another granite workers predominate, rendering the street white with fine stone chips. On Temple street, you remark temples of different Buddhist denominations, standing side by side in good fellowship; and in Fishmongers' alley all the houses have fish-stalls, and are filled with the odor of fish. The Japanese do not keep house in one place and store in another; they live in their stores. Neither do we have that singular system of boarding houses. Our people have homes of their own, however poor.

My family lived on the main street, which is divided into four subdivisions or "blocks." The second block is the commercial centre, so to speak, of the town, and there my father kept a store. My grandfather, I understood, resided in another street before he moved with his son-in-law, my father, to the main street. He lived to the great age of eighty; I shall always remember him with honor and respect. Of my grandmother I know absolutely nothing, she having passed away before I was born.

It is customary in Japan that a man too old for business and whose head is white with the effect of many weary winters, should retire and hibernate in a quiet chamber, or in a cottage called inkyo (hiding place), and be waited upon by his eldest son or son-in-law who succeeds him in business. My good grandfather—his kindly face and pleasant words come back to me this moment—lived in a nice little house in the rear of my father's. Although strong in mind he was bent with age and went about with the help of a bamboo cane. He lived alone, had little to do, but read a great deal, and thought much, and when tired did some light manual work. It was a great pleasure for me to visit him often. In cold winter days he would be found sitting by kotatsu, a native heating apparatus. It is constructed on the following plan: a hole a foot square is cut in the centre of the matted floor, wherein a stone vessel is fitted, and a frame of wood about a foot high laid on it so as to protect the quilt that is to be spread over it, from burning. The vessel is filled with ashes, and a charcoal fire is burned in it. I used to take my position near my grandfather, with my hands and feet beneath the quilt, and ask him to tell stories. My feet were either bare or in a pair of socks, for before getting on the floor we leave our shoes in the yard. Our shoes, by the way, are more like the ancient Jewish sandals than the modern leather shoes.

In this little house of my grandfather's I erected my own private shrine of Tenjinsan, the god of penmanship. The Japanese and the Chinese value highly a skilful hand at writing; a famous-scroll-writer gets a large sum of money with a few strokes of his brush; he is looked up to like a celebrated painter. We school-boys occasionally proposed penmanship contests. On the same sheet of paper each of us wrote, one beside another, his favorite character, or did his best at one character we had mutually agreed upon, and took it to our teacher to decide upon the finest hand. The best specimens of a school are sometimes framed and hung on the walls of a public temple of Tenjin. He is worshiped by all school-boys, and I also followed the fashion. My image of him was made of clay; I laid it on a shelf and offered saké (rice-wine) in two tiny earthen bottles, lighted a little lamp every night and put up prayers in childish zeal. The family rejoiced at my devotion; they finally bought me, one holiday, a miniature toy temple. It was painted in gay colors; I was delighted with it beyond expression, and my devotion increased tenfold.

## CHAPTER II.

The earliest recollection I have of my school life is my entrance with a number of playmates into a private gentleman's school. At that time the common school system which now exists in Japan had not been adopted; some gentlemen of the town kept private schools, in which exercises consisted mainly of penmanship; for arithmetic we had to go somewhere else. In Imabari there lived a keen-eyed little man who was wonderfully quick at figures, and to him we repaired for instruction in mathematics. We worked, not with slate and pencil, but with a rectangular wooden frame set with beads, resembling an abacus. It is called soroban; you find it in every store in Japan. I like it better than slate and pencil, for the fundamental operations of arithmetic, but cannot use it in higher mathematics. I remember seeing a young man of my acquaintance perform algebraic calculations, of which we had some knowledge before the influx of Western learning, with a number of little black and white blocks called the " mathematical blocks." A knowledge of penmanship and arithmetic is all that is required of a man of business, but a learned man is expected to read Chinese.

My schoolmaster was a kind of priest, not of Buddhism nor of Shintoism, but one of those who go by the name of Yamabushi; he let his hair grow instead of shaving it off as the Buddhist priest does, wore high clogs and the peculiar robe of his religion. He simply followed his father in the vocation; he was a young man of high promise and manifested more ardor in letters than at the prayers for the sick or for the prosperity of the people. His house was on the fourth block of the main street, set back a little from the street and with an open yard between the tall, elaborate gate and the mansion. The front of the residence was taken up by the shrine; the school was kept in the back part of the house. When we first entered the school we were known as the "newcomers" among the older boys, and though bullying was not altogether absent, we had no ordeal to go through as the Freshmen have in American colleges.

The pupil's equipment in one of these old-fashioned schools consisted of a low table, a cushion to squat upon, and a chest for the following articles: white paper, copy-books and a small box containing a stone ink-vessel, a cake of india ink, an earthen water-bottle and brushes. A little water is poured in the hollow of the stone vessel, the india ink rubbed on it for a while, and when the water becomes sufficiently black the brush is dipped in it. Then looking at model characters written down for us in a separate book by the teacher, we try to trace the same on our copy-books, paying close attention to every particular. The first that we must learn is our alphabet of forty-eight letters.

I recall vividly the trials in making the alphabetical figures. I tried time and again, but to fail; the sorrow gathered thickly in my mind and soon the grief overpowered all my strenuous efforts not to weep, then the master would send one of the older boys to help me. He stands behind me while I sit, grasps my hand which holds the brush, and to my heart's content traces figures like the master's in perfection.

The copy-book is made of the tenacious soft Japanese paper, many sheets of which are bound together. Each of the forty-eight characters is studied separately; it is written large so that the learner may see where a bold stroke is required and where a mild touch. After the alphabet we learn to write Chinese characters. The copy-books become black after a while, being dried and used again; therefore they need not be perfectly white at first; usually they are made of the sheets of an old ledger. I used to see on the pages of the copy-books made for me by my father, old debts and credits, and the names of the parties concerned in them, dating back to grandfather's time; they disappeared collectively under my wild dash and sweep of india ink. What an act of generosity to wipe out the remembrance of former money complications! After a day's work all the copy-books are literally drenched with the black fluid; they are moist and heavy. They must be dried. Every patch of sunshine about the school is improved, every breezy corner turned to account. At home the kitchen is spread with them at night, so as to have them dry by the morning. Copy-books that have done long service are coated with a smooth, shining incrustation of carbon—shining if good ink has been used, but dull if ink is of cheap quality. The quality of an india ink cake is not only judged by its lustre, but also by its hardness and odor; a good one is hard and pleasant and the bad soft and unpleasant. After we have practised writing the letters for some time, we finally write them on white papers and present them to our teacher, who with red ink makes further necessary corrections. If the final copy is satisfactory, he sets us at work on a next portion.

Every morning, after breakfast, I gathered together dried copy-books and went after or waited for some boys to come along. We strolled up the street toward the schoolmaster's, calling on other boys as we went. The first task in school upon our arrival was to set the tables in order, get the things out of the chests and go after some water for making the ink. It was no comfortable occupation, cold winter mornings, to get the water from the well in the windy, open yard in the rear of the house, and dip our hand and the drip-bottle together and keep them in it until all the air escaped by bubbles, and the bottle was full. A bottle though I called it, the receptacle is a hollow, square china vessel, with two small holes on the flat surface—one in the centre and the other in one of the corners.

We sit in a house where there is practically no arrangement for heating and where we are poorly protected from the gusts from without. The Japanese house is built opening widely into the external air; it has but a few segments of external walls around it; therefore one can select no breezier abode during the warm months, but in the dead of win er— the mere thought of it makes me shiver. Those immense open spaces could be closed, to be sure, at night with solid pine-board sliding doors; but in the daytime the question of light comes in. To meet this difficulty our ingenious forefathers had contrived a frame-work of wood pasted with paper. You must know they had no idea of glass. We can scarcely call it a happy solution of the problem, for the paper is soon punched through and lets in the biting wind. Too much active ventilation takes place, whistling through the holes; and then when a storm strikes us, the whole frail work shakes in the grooves wherein its two ends are fitted, like the chattering of the teeth. This sliding paper partition is called shoji, and of late has been somewhat replaced by the more expensive glass windows. Since the introduction of glass I have seen the shoji partly covered with it and partly with paper, the Japanese thinking it very convenient to see through the partition without being at the pains of pushing it aside or making a hole in the paper. Had paper been entirely discarded and glass alone been used the Japanese house would be much brighter and warmer.

Such a building is a poor place to hold a school in, but the boys were used to it and they behaved so— quarreling, weeping, laughing, shrieking—that there was little time left for them to feel the cold in their young warm blood.

## CHAPTER III.

When just from school our faces and hands were as black as demons' with ink. On my reaching home my mother would take care of the copy-books, and send me straight to the kitchen to wash before I sat down to the table. The vessel corresponding to the basin is made of brass. We have not learned to use soap; old folks believe that it would turn our black hair red like that of the foreigners. There is no convenience of faucet or pump; each house has its own well in the back yard, even in the city;—hence no water-works, no gas-works, and no fuss about plumbing; the housewife must proceed to the well for water, rain or shine, and struggle back to the kitchen with a pailful of it every time she needs it.

The kitchen itself is not often floored; the range (of clay and of different appearance from that which is used here) and the sink stand directly on mother earth under a shed-like roof which has been darkened by smoke. The range has no chimney; not coal but wood is burned in it, and all the smoke escapes from the front opening or mouth and fills the entire kitchen, causing the dear black eyes of the amiable housewife to suffuse with tears.

She has the small Japanese towel wrapped round

her head to protect the elaborate coiffure from the soot of years, that has accumulated everywhere and falls in gentle flakes, snow-fashion, on things universally. She works her pair of lungs at the "fire-blowing tube," a large bamboo two or three feet long, opened at one end for a mouth-piece and punched at the other for a narrow orifice. The imprisoned volumes of smoke in the kitchen must crowd out through a square aperture in the roof; if it be closed on a rainy day, they must escape through windows or crevices the best they may.

The water when brought in from the well is emptied into a deep heavy earthen reservoir of reddish hue standing near the sink. With a wooden ladle I would dip out the water into the brass basin (sheet brass, not solid), and wash myself without soap in the most rapid manner possible, yearning eagerly for dinner. The towel is a piece of cotton dyed blue with designs left undyed or dyed black. I grumbled, I confess, when my mother sent me back for a more thorough washing; but with the utmost alacrity I always saluted the very sight of viands.

Oftentimes I was late and was obliged to eat a late dinner alone; but when all of our family sat down together, enough of life was manifested. At one end my witty young brother provoked laughter in us with stuff and nonsense; next him sat my younger sister, quiet and good. I assumed my position between my sister and my father and mother, who sat together at the head of the row. I forget to mention that my elder brother, whose place must be next above me, had been ordered to keep peace in the region of my merry little brother. My sister-in-law or my elder brother's wife took her stand opposite us, surrounded by a rice-bucket, a cast-iron cooking-pot, a teapot, a basket of rice-bowls, saucers, etc. She it was who had to cook and serve dinner and wash dishes and take care of her babies. It is this that renders a young married woman's lot in life very hard in Japan, the princicipal weight of daily work devolving upon her. After all this, if parents-in-law are not pleased with her she is in imminent danger of being turned off like a hired servant, however affectionate she may be toward her husband; and the husband feels it his duty to part with her despite his deep attachment; so sacred is regarded the manifestation of filial piety! Fortunately for my sister-in-law, my mother, who has four daughters living with their husbands' relatives, made every household task as light and easy as she could for her and expressed sympathy when needed, knowing that her own daughters were laboring in the like circumstances.

We do not eat at one large dining table with chairs round it; we sit on our heels on the matted floor with a separate small table in front of each of us. I remember my table was in the form of a box about a foot square, the lid of which I lifted and laid on the body of the box with the inner surface up. The inner surface was japanned red, the outer surface and the sides of the box green. The convenience of this form of table is, that you can store away your own rice-bowl, vegetable-dish and chopstick case in the box. Some tables stand on two flat and broad legs, others have drawers in their sides. We do not ring the bell in announcing dinner; in large families they clap two oblong blocks of hard wood. Grace before meat was a thing unknown to us; my brother, however, had a queer habit of bowing to his chopsticks at the close of meals. He did it from simple heartfelt gratitude and not for show. In his ignorance of Him who provideth our daily bread, he concluded to return thanks to the tools of immediate usefulness. Chopsticks are of various materials—bamboo, mahogany, ivory, etc.,—and in different shapes—round, angular, slender at one end and stout at the other, etc. In a great public feast where there is no knowing the number present, or a religious fête where reverential cleanliness is formally insisted upon, fork-shaped splints of soft wood are distributed among the guests who rend them asunder into pairs of impromptu chopsticks. On the morning of New Year's Day tradition requires us to use chopsticks prepared hastily of mulberry twigs in handling rice-paste cakes called mochi, which the people cook with various edibles and eat, as a sort of religious ceremony.

Rice is the staple food. Vegetables and fishes are also consumed, yet no meat is eaten. Partridge and game, however, were sanctioned from early times as food or rather as luxuries. To cook rice just right—not too soft nor too hard—is not an easy matter; it is considered an art every Japanese maiden of marriageable age must needs acquire. The rice is first washed in a wooden tub, and then transferred to a deep iron cooking-pot with some water. The point lies in the question, how much water is needed? Neither too much nor too little; there is a golden mean. If the rice be cooked either the very least little bit soft or hard the young servant-wife, for really that she is, is blamed for it. The right amount of water is only ascertained by trial. No less puzzling is the degree of heat to be applied to the pot, and the point at which to withdraw the fuel and leave the cooking to be completed without any further application of heat. These things I speak of not merely from observation but from personal experience. When I was off at a boarding school, which I may have occasion to speak of, I experimented in boarding myself for a while; I learned there how to cook as at a young ladies' seminary, as well as how to write and read.

Hot boiled rice we always have at dinner; at supper and breakfast we pour boiling tea over cold rice in the bowl and are content. Tea is boiling in the kitchen from morning till night. It is drunk with no sugar or milk; indeed, the scrupulous inhabitants of the "land of the gods" never dreamt of tasting the milk of a brute. If a babe is nourished with cow's milk, it is believed that the horns will grow on his forehead. When no palatable dishes are to be had we eat our rice with pickled plums and preserved radishes, turnips, egg-plants and cabbage. The preserves are not done up in glass jars; they are kept in a huge tub of salt and rice-bran. During the summer months when vegetables are plenty and cheap we buy a great quantity of them from a farmer of our acquaintance. He brings them on the back of a horse. The poor animal is usually loaded so heavily that only his head and tail are visible amidst the mountain of cabbage leaves. Days are spent in washing and scrubbing the roots and bulbs of the garden, many more in drying them in the sun. House-tops, weather-beaten walls, fences and all available windy corners are utilized in hanging up the vegetables. When partly dried they are packed in salt and rice-bran and subjected to pressure in bamboo-hooped wooden tubs, commonly by laying old millstones on them. Being but partially dry, the vegetables deliver the remaining moisture to the powder in which they are packed, and in course of time the whole contents become soaked in a yellowish, muddy, pungent liquid. Kōkŏ, as the vegetables are then called, can be preserved in this way throughout the whole year. They are taken out from time to time, washed and sliced and relished with great satisfaction. They are something that is sure to be obtained in any house at any time; with cold rice and hot tea they make up our simplest fare.

When I was late from school I made out my dinner with the rice and kōkŏ. Frequently, however, my provident mother set aside for me something nice.

## CHAPTER IV.

I BELIEVE we had no afternoon session in the old-fashioned school; and the boys had two or three pet games to play in leisure hours. One of them was played in this manner: each one is provided with a number of pointed iron sticks a few inches long. The leader pitches one of his sticks in soft soil; the second follows suit, aiming to root out his predecessor's by the force of pitching in his own close to it; then the third, the fourth, and all around the company. Another of the games was played with square chips of wood, on which were painted heads of men, demons and all sorts of fanciful figures. A triangle was drawn on hard level ground and at a distance from its base a parallel line; from which line the boys each in turn threw a common lot of the chips, contributed by all, into the inside of the triangle. It must be done with the same nicety of aim and attitude as in throwing quoits. A habit established itself among us of the players coming down to the ground on all fours immediately after the act of throwing; it was the consequence of bending too far forward in order to get in all the chips at the peril of neglecting the centre of gravity. The chips that flew outside of the triangle were gathered by the next player and those in the inside allowed to be taken by the player, should he be able to throw a chip from his hand and lay it on them one by one. If he failed at any moment, the next player gathered together all the remaining chips and played his turn. A modification of this game consists in throwing the chips against a wall, and counting good those only that remain inside a straight line parallel with the foot of the wall, and turning over to the next player those on the outside. The game is played by girls as well as by boys, although they rarely play together.

We also used to play hide-and-seek, blind-man's-buff and other games that are familiar in this country.

Later in my school days the government underwent great changes, and it adopted the common school system of the West. My father was to pay a school-tax and I to attend a new school, where instruction was not in penmanship alone but extended over various subjects. Text-books on arithmetic, Japanese geography and history had been compiled after the American pattern, but no grammar appeared; the educational department left the language to be taught by the purely inductive method. The fact is that the Japanese language has not been systematized; should one attempt it he would find it a tremendous task.

When I was on the point of leaving for America my brother put into my hand a Japanese grammar in two thin volumes, written by a literary man in Tokio, and said that it was being used in schools. I have them still by me and privately consider the attempt not a very great success. The gentleman tries to follow the steps of the European grammarian; he cleverly makes out "noun" and "pronoun," "verb" and "adverb"— even "article," (which, in good faith, I never in the slightest suspected our language was guilty of possessing) from the chaos. Upon the whole, the book has the effect of confusing instead of enlightening me; after my dabbling in languages, in Japanese I prefer to be taught like a babe.

Japanese dictionaries are for the purpose of hunting up Japanese meanings of Chinese letters, answering to your Latin and Greek lexicons. So much of Chinese has been introduced into our language in the course of centuries, that it is now impossible to read one line in a Japanese newspaper, for instance, without coming across Chinese characters. In books for women and children and in popular novels Japanese equivalents are written beside Chinese words. In getting lessons we made little use of the dictionaries; once learned by dictation from the teacher we relied on our memory and that of others; hence frequent review was needed to retain them. As the new school system took root, the school books began to have vocabularies and keys; and the Chinese classics pursued by advanced students their "pony."

Just at present a movement is on foot to simplify our tongue in its complication with Chinese. People generally suppose the two languages are alike; many of them have asked me if I could interpret to them what the down-town "washees" were so merrily babbling about over their flatirons. It is a mistake; Japanese and Chinese are totally different, strange as it may appear. And yet I had to learn my Chinese in order to read our standard works. If the common people could understand Chinese as well as the learned persons, I believe we could get along very well with our language as it is; but they do not. It would be very inconvenient indeed if, for instance, in this country the "educated" people should use long words all the while, or employ French expressions freely in talking and writing. Just such a pedantry exists in my native country, and truly educated men are crying out for reformation. There are two parties. One party thinks it can do it by using unadulterated Japanese, while the other deems nothing short of the Romanization of the whole fabric—that is, the adoption of the Roman alphabet in spelling Japanese words—could accomplish the end. Opinion is equally divided between them; the second party may appear slightly stronger on account of its members for the greater part being students of other languages beside their own. Both these parties issue periodicals to advocate their theories and at the same time to carry their ideas into practice. These are worthy efforts; as yet they are experiments. We are told that the growth of a language is a matter of generations, that language has life like everything else, and that it must undergo changes despite feeble human efforts.

But to return. Happily our former schoolmaster was hired by the new organization and still took charge of us. He was a gifted young gentleman, a writer of lucid sentences and also something of a poet. He encouraged us greatly in polishing our Japanese-Chinese composition. It was his custom to select the best composition from the class, on a given subject, copy it on the blackboard and point out before the class what elegant epithets could be substituted for vulgar ones. It was a pleasure with him to do this, whereas in mathematics he did not show much zeal. Above all, he inherited from his father the art of fine penmanship. His brother, too, had a well-formed hand quite like our teacher's; evidently it was a case of hereditary genius.

At times our beloved master voluntarily offered to recite to us records of famous battles and heroes that adorn the pages of Japanese history. He did this from the love of telling them; the boys were as fond of hearing as he was of telling. He had in hand no book to help him; the gallant exploits of the brave and handsome, the rescuing of the virtuous fair, the crash, dash and rush of horses, lances and swords he called up from memory and decked with his teeming imagination. On such an occasion his language was prolific, his voice modulated according to the shifting shades of the subject matter; in short, his whole man, heart and soul, went to the making of the story. His eyes and expression! they often told half his story. Many a time the bells surprised us at the midst of his soul-stirring recital, and suddenly called us back to the unromantic light of modern day and to the homely exercises of school. The stories were told to us serially, in the hours of intermission and were a sort of optional course. They were so popular that very few were found playing about the grounds when the eloquent romancer proceeded in his narrative.

Yet he was not a man of weak indulgence toward the boys; his sense of duty was equally strong. If a youngster was seen undertaking to do anything naughty he would give him a stern look, his cheeks were inflated, his eyes showed the white plainly. The whole room was then silent as a tomb. But if a fun-loving fellow ventured, perhaps, to thrust out his little tongue roguishly or let out a giggle behind his hand, then the teacher irresistibly relaxed the corners of his mouth, and in another moment the hall rang with the hilarious laughter of reconciliation and good-fellowship.

Later I came under the instruction of different masters, but he it was who led me in infancy so carefully by the hand, as it were, to the first step of the ladder of knowledge, and he it will be who shall remain the longest in my memory.

At school the common mode of punishment was to let the culprit stand erect a whole hour together, facing his own class or a class in an adjoining room. Although no dunce-cap was on his head, a roomful of staring eyes struck a burning shame into his soul. Nevertheless, urchins there were who considered it a supreme delight to be taken off the troublesome exercises and carried to the next room on a visit, where they had made many acquaintances at a previous banishment. Indeed, they had become so inured to it that they thought nothing of it afterward.

Once the whole school, except a few good children, incurred the teachers' displeasure. I have forgotten what the offence was; all were prevented from going home after school and ordered to stand up till dark, each with a bowl full of water. There they stood like a regiment of begging saints with the bowls in the outstretched arms, which if they moved the water ran over the brim, and the delinquents would have been whipped. At first we thought it capital fun, because so many were in company to commiserate; we laughed aloud, bobbed and courtesied to the teachers in mockery; but in time we had to change our minds. The result of standing still like a statue began to tell upon us; our limbs began to ache and feel stiff; the jolliest member gave a cowardly sob; and the patient fellow in the corner, hitherto unnoticed, attracted public attention by dropping the burden. The china went to pieces. He blubbered out, as if that was sufficient apology. Through the intercession of some kindly folk we finally came home to supper and comfort.

We were continually threatened with another method of punishment, though I doubt if the teachers would have inflicted it on us. It was an intolerably cruel one: the offender was compelled to stand up with a lighted bundle of senkoes until it burned down close to his hand. The senko is a slender incense stick burned before the shrine of Buddha and of our ancestors, and manufactured by kneading a certain aromatic powder to a paste and squeezing it out into innumerable very slim, extremely fragile, brownish rods. When dry, these are gathered into good-sized bundles and put in the market. A few cents will buy you more senkoes than you need. As the bundle burns away slowly—slowly to prolong the agony, the fire encroaches on the skin and the flesh. Unless the offender surrenders himself to the heartless will of his pedagogue he must suffer injury from the heat. This punishment was actually in practice in old days when the tyrannical masters had their way, but went out of fashion at the dawn of civilization.

Our teachers carried flexible sticks, which they played with while teaching, or used in pointing at the maps; they never whipped anybody with them to my knowledge; but in going their rounds among the pupils, if any were engaged in conversation or in any way inattentive, flogged the table before them in such a manner as to cause the poor fellows to jump into the air.

## CHAPTER V.

WHEN the close of a day called me home from school, and my father's work was done, a sense of contentment and repose brooded over our household. A vigorous scrub at a public bath often gave our tired bodies a renewed muscular tone. I accompanied my father to this resort; when I was very young, my mother carried me thither. The bath-house is a private establishment of its proprietor, and public in the sense that townspeople betake themselves to it without restraint. The charge is only a few mills for the adult, half the amount for the child and nothing for the suckling. If a number of checks (branded, flat pieces of wood) be purchased at one time, the average charge is still less. In Imabari, there are a dozen or more of these baths; they mostly occupy the corners of the streets like American drug stores. They are opened from late in the afternoon till late at night; on holidays accommodation baths are ready at early daybreak. As soon as a bath is in readiness, its keeper places a flag at the eaves, in the daytime, and a square, paper lantern after dusk. At the entrance is a stand, where you deposit your fare, and exchange a word on the weather with the keeper if you are neighborly. Advancing a few steps, you leave your clogs on a low platform, on the sides of which rise tiers of lockers for clothes. You must bring your own towels; ladies also take with them little cotton bags of rice-bran. They close the bags tightly with strings, soak them in hot water and rub their faces and hands with the wet balls. The process is said to refine the texture of the skin wonderfully.

The bath proper is a great, covered tank, full of hot water, with a terrace-work of planks sloping down on the four sides, where you sit and wash. The ceiling is low enough to bump your head unless you are cautious; it projects forward and stoops to prevent the steam from escaping unnecessarily; therefore, even when it is lighted within, it is twilight, owing to the confined vapor. One feels in it as if working in a mine or tunnel. Older men discuss town topics and business, and young men hum popular airs as they bathe, and intimate friends press each other to rub down their backs. The water is kept warm by a huge metallic heater behind, which is in communication with the tank but covered with planks so as not to scald the bathers' feet. In case the water proves too hot, the bathers consult each other's comfort courteously, and one of them claps his hands. It is answered by a sound at the entrance stand, and immediately cold water spouts into the tank. Then the men stir the tank thoroughly on all sides. Being but a child I took great delight in the excitement. I would creep up to the hole and plug it with my wet towel, and after a few minutes pull it out abruptly to see the water spurt forth with redoubled energy. The wall has usually a small door; pushing it open the fireman peeps in occasionally, when there is too much noise. The first time I noticed it, I was almost scared out of my wits; for, happening to look around, I saw on the dim wall a grim human head staring me in the face.

Between the tank and the floor is a space paved with large, flat, rectangular stones and cemented with mortar, where the people who think it too close in the tank can step out and wash, sitting on long, narrow benches; in some baths this place is overlaid with planks in such a manner that water can trickle down between them. Here we may use soap, but not in the tank. Several small wooden tubs are near at hand; with them we pour the hot water over our body after rubbing, and in them we give our towels a final clean-water washing when through using them. The clear, cold water for the latter purpose is constantly bubbling up in a shallow, well-like enclosure hard by. A couple of dippers float in it, and the people also drink of the water, if thirsty. In well-regulated baths, near the cold-water enclosure is a hot water cistern, constantly fed through a bamboo pipe with boiling water that has not been used. People of cleanly habits, on emerging from the common tank, dip out this fresh, warm water and bathe again. Of course, it would be objectionable to retain the same water in the tank all day and have people bathe in it over and over; as a matter of fact, a portion of it is drawn off at intervals and replaced with a fresh supply.

The ladies' side is precisely the same in arrangement as the gentlemen's; a partition, however, separates them completely.

If you meet a man on the street in Japan with a wet towel hanging on his shoulder, he is from the public bath. He wears no hat even in sallying forth into the open air from the confined atmosphere, walks leisurely along, dragging the high clogs and feeling thoroughly comfortable. In summer evenings, while maidens, mothers and children are cooling themselves in the breeze on movable platforms in front of their residences, young men from the bath come strolling up, inquire politely after their health and make themselves agreeable. As the after-bath garment and towel are to be thus exhibited before the eyes of their admirers new fashions arise every year in regard to them. The fashion changes not so much in tailoring as in the color and pattern.

We are not without private baths, too. Large aristocratic families are all provided with them. The bath-house is usually fitted up in a wing at the back of the building; in it a tub large enough to admit a person in a squatting position is placed on a caldron. The loose wooden bottom of the tub is left floating while the water boils, serving as the cover; it is fastened afterward. The head of the family goes in first; after him, his wife; then come their children, beginning with the eldest; after them follow the domestics, ranged according to their relative importance.

Evenings at home were always spent very pleasantly, especially before my sisters were married and went away. There were four of them, excluding the eldest who had left us a good while ago, but used to visit us, and add to our gayety. What did we do to enjoy ourselves? We had music and dancing very often, singing, of course, parties to which our best friends came, games of cards, social chat and fireside talk—whatever goes to make home attractive. Mother took great interest in them herself; she chaperoned the girls—we had young ladies of the neighborhood come to us, and our house was looked upon as one of the social foci of little Imabari. But a reverse in my father's fortune and frequent change of abode put an end to those happy days of yore.

Japanese dancing, I declare without prejudice, is more elaborate and graceful than your round and square dances, but may not be as fascinating; ladies and gentlemen do not dance together. Moreover, our dancing is not anything that can be picked up at balls and receptions, nor is it learned by hopping and skipping at the dancing academy. In fact, it is not the simple keeping time with music, not repetitions of the same steps over and over again; it is composed of posturing and is more like acting, though the manœuvres are predetermined, in regular order, and not left to the dancer's fancy. Here in America dancing is easily acquired by persons who have an ear for music and grace of carriage, and after having learned to waltz "elegantly" or "divinely" they have practically mastered all other figures. In Japan, each figure is emphatically a new one, and there are many, many figures with distinct names;

one cannot learn them all—each figure requires a separate effort for its mastery. A dance lasts twenty minutes or more; scarcely two steps in it seem alike. In learning a Japanese dance one begins with little tosses of the head, engaging sways of the body and easy movements of the extremities.

Many young girls of the town practised the primary exercises in our house; they came to ask assistance of my second sister, who excelled the rest in dancing. I see her vivacious figure trip up to a beginner, who struck an awkward attitude, and correct a twist of the neck as the barber and the photographer fix their customers' heads. She taught my youngest sister very thoroughly in all the dances she knew, and after that mother put Mitsu (that is the name of my little sister) under the special tuition of a lady who had just then arrived from Osaka, a great centre of enjoyment and politeness. The dancing mistress had a very pretty adopted daughter who assisted her, and they together aroused enthusiasm among the people of Imabari in the art of grace. A society formed itself naturally with the lady as the nucleus, and a scheme was projected for a public exhibition of dances. The parents of the dancing children manifested more zeal than the children themselves. As they came in for it with willing heart and liberal hand, the scheme was pushed forward with surprising rapidity. A mammoth curtain was made that was to be hoisted in the theatre where the brilliant events were to take place; it had painted on it numerous big fans, and on the fans were written the names of the members. My big brother was busily engaged in painting scenes and constructing apparatus, my sisters were diligently selecting stage dresses for Mitsu. And then the young ladies met in our place to rehearse the dances, songs and instrumental music, that made us still more agreeably busy. Weeks were spent in preparation; and when it came off at last, the entertainment was a grand affair continuing for several days; the town turned out in a body. It was more like successful theatricals than anything, and was repeated once or twice afterwards, with the substitution for the former dances of many equally classical pieces.

All the dances are accompanied by songs and instruments. The instrument most commonly used is the samisen; it looks somewhat like a banjo, but is much larger and has a square body instead of a round one; the wood-work is of mahogany. In playing it the touching is not done with the fingers, but with a plectrum of ivory. The samisen is capable of giving out both the mellow notes of the guitar and the sharp tone-sprays of the banjo. You hear it played in Japanese homes to the same extent as the piano is in this country. We had in our family two or three samisens, and every day my sisters practised on them.

Other instruments of music are the koto, the tsuzumi and the drum. The koto is a heavy, thirteen-stringed instrument, of which by mere description I can hardly give an idea. The player sits before it, and with claws fitted to the fingers of both hands plays at the two ends. The tsuzumi is an hour-glass-shaped drum which is tapped with the right hand. Two tsuzumis are frequently played by a single person; a light tsuzumi is laid on the right shoulder and held by the left hand, and a heavy tsuzumi is rested on the left knee slightly elevated and pressed down with the left elbow; the right hand is free to move between the two tsuzumis which it beats. The light tsuzumi emits a soft tone, the heavy one a deep sound. The stroke, unless skillfully performed, often inflicts a violent injury to the fingers. The vellum of the tsuzumi is of fox skin and yellow in color, that of the samisen is of cat skin and white as snow. The drum is not the sort drubbed in a military band; it is smaller and more moderate in its intonation.

These instruments,—the koto, samisen, taiko (drum) and tsuzumi are frequently played in concert; the samisen players—two of them, at any rate, to one of the others—sing in high pitch while their supple fingers twinkle across the chords; the taiko and tsuzumi beaters shriek now and then as they thrum and whack. Do I like it? Isn't it hideous? Well, I can't say how it would strike me now; yet I used to think it all very fine.

There is another stringed instrument, a ridiculously simple one that I liked best. It is named ichigecckin. A plain board, a few feet in length, and a few inches in width, with no other ornament than half a dozen Chinese characters written on it to indicate the various keys; only a single string along the whole length; a bamboo ring for the middle finger of the left hand to touch on the keys; and a small flat piece of horn to pick the string with: these make up an ichigecckin. The origin of this unpretentious instrument is said to be as follows: a high court noble of amiable disposition and poetic temperament on his way southward from the ancient palace in Kioto, years ago, was obliged to moor near the beautiful shores of Akashi on account of a heavy storm. The sea tossed about his boat; the sky stretched gray; the thatch overhead became soaked in the rain; the wind sighed among the pines on the deserted shore. A sense of loneliness weighed on his gentle nature. The fading landscape in the dusk, the mournful cry of a sea-gull, the sight of a boat miles away laboring in the waves, peradventure laden with lives—all conspired to produce in him a sadness more than human. In order to beguile his ennui, he constructed himself a rude musical instrument with a board and string, and poured out the feelings of the hour in many a celebrated tune. The ichigecckin music is low and simple and sweet. On rainy nights, when the candle burns dim and all is quiet, I feel most in the mood to listen.

Japanese music is in a crude state of development; there are no written notes to go by in playing, nor in singing is there any system like your "Do, Re, Mi, etc," to depend upon. As yet it is strictly an art and not a science; one is obliged to get it by observation, imitation and practice. Music is taught by lady teachers; but a set of blind men, who perform massage for a livelihood, take scholars, likewise. They have their heads shaved, walk abroad alone, feeling their way with sticks; some of them have been to Osaka and Kioto for a musical degree, conferred on them in certain schools. In Japan music is not divided into the vocal and the instrumental; the two are always taught together by the same instructor.

Vocal cultivation is conducted in a singular way. During the winter the girl in training clothes herself comfortably, takes a samisen and ascends every cold night the scaffold erected on the roof of the house for drying purposes. There she sits for hours together amid the howling blasts, singing defiantly and banging away courageously at the samisen. Upon her coming down, she is found worse than hoarse; she can hardly utter a word. The training is observed persistently until her former voice has entirely left her and gradually a clear new voice, as it were, breaks out in the harshness. This voice can stand a storm. The discipline is now over, a little care needs only to be exercised in the maintenance of the acquired voice. The practice, I am well aware, will hardly commend itself to the gentlewomen of this republic, who are wrapped all winter long in furs and sealskins and would not think for a moment of leaving the chimney corner. In my fancy I hear them repel it with their passionate "What an idea!" Therefore, I conclude it prudent to say nothing in praise of the barbarous measure, and simply state the plain fact that it has produced many an Apollo in Japan. In the other seasons of the year, after having screamed out her worthless voice, the girl takes a dose of pulverized ginger and sugar to tone up the vocal chords.

I digressed from dancing to music; now I wish to return to dancing again for a few moments. In parlor gatherings and sociables light pieces are presented; and such small things as fans, towels, masks, umbrellas, bells, tambourines only are used in dancing. Fans are most commonly used, many astonishing tricks being played with them. The guests sit in a body off the arena, where the dancer steps out; the samisen player tunes the instrument on one side. The preliminary chords ring; then come the words in song, and in accordance with them the actions of the dancer. The dances intended for the stage are much more elaborate. Scenes are to be fitted up; varieties of gew-gaws,— artificial flowers, falling paper snow, fallen woolly-cotton snow, painted waves, the outline of a boat, a lantern moon, a gilded paper crown, baskets, shells, a wooden scythe, a toy tub, high clogs, yards of white silk, etc., etc.,—are to be procured. These vain, empty articles rise up in my mind, for I used to see them stowed away in the dusty garret. They were jostled about by other things, lay in everybody's way, became mutilated, and fully repaid the glory they had received one night behind the foot-lights. We have spent time and money in getting them up, however; certain things we have even sent for to Osaka or Kioto. I remember seeing my sister practise day after day dancing with the aforementioned long white silk scarfs. The dance was to represent the process of bleaching by a famous maiden (named Okané) who dwelt beside Lake Biwa. Of all sorts of waves and undulations and flutterings she had to produce with them I recollect one:—it is to shake one scarf right and left horizontally overhead, and the other up and down longitudinally in front. Try it with your hands and see, reader; you will find it no easy task. In the stage dances the dancers must dress true to the conceptions of the characters they undertake to represent. This necessitates a large wardrobe, though the gorgeous costumes are generally made of cheap materials, and the aid of artificial lights is expected to finish off the effects. The face of the dancer is usually painted, but not so much so as that of a professional actress. The whole affair, however, savors strongly of stage-play. Several persons sometimes dance together, carry on dialogues and, indeed, dance part of a play or drama.

## CHAPTER VI.

Our best friends were not limited to ladies, but comprised several select gentlemen. In Japan we have more social freedom than people are apt to think. Many of the young gentlemen entertained us well. Some were beautiful singers, others fine musicians, and still others elegant dancers. One among them, a person of fine appearance who fell in love with the dancing teacher's pretty daughter and who afterward married her, was quite highly accomplished. He possessed artistic tastes, probably inherited from his father, who was an art connoisseur—art, as it appeared in china wares, scrolls, kakemonoes (wall hangings), old bric-à-brac, etc. The young man could sketch, talk brilliantly, render gentlemen's dances creditably, and was handsome to look at. He used to pay us respects, for his parents, particularly his cheery bright-eyed little mother, was a dear friend of ours, and his sisters were great friends of my sisters. The girls went to sewing school together. You know, as we do not have the sewing machine and as we are to a certain extent our own tailors and dressmakers, Japanese girls must take lessons in sewing, as American young ladies take lessons in painting and on the piano. They do "crazy"

work and fancy work, too, and talk over their
notions extravagantly, rashly confide everything
to each other, and exclaim "lovely!" in Japanese.

This young man felt from his childhood a passion
for the stage. As he grew up his dramatic taste
became irresistible; at last, escaping the vigilance
of his family, he ran away to the neighboring province of Tosa (ours is Iyo), and committed himself
to the care of a noted actor named Hanshirō. The
young man told us how he had been launched in
the work; the actor-apprentice, when admitted to
the stage, is obliged to put on rags and help make
up the mob or a gang of thieves. In order to make
a hero's power appear greater by contrast, it is a
stage trick in Japan that the mob, thieves, and
characters of that sort should turn somersaults at
the hero's simple lifting of his hand. It is a sight
to be seen when a swarm of them around one brave
person turn in the air and light safely upon their
feet; they do it so very deftly that they must practice a great deal. Our friend first practiced the acro-
batic feat on a thick quilt for fear that he might
break his neck. In time, however, he could do it
on the hard wooden stage floor. After filling this
gymnastic rôle for some time, he was promoted by
degrees to more important posts. By reason of his
personal attractions he was at his best as a gallant
youth. I have observed many a fair spectator
flush visibly, heave gentle sighs and watch him in
absorption while he delivered a love soliloquy in a
clear voice.

He did become an actor in the fullest sense of the
term and a creditable one, too; but having satisfied

his long cherished desire for once (a space of several years), he obeyed the paternal summons and returned home. He then went into business and fairly settled down to earnest life. Nevertheless, at times his roving nature got the better of him, and the young man would be missed from home. Soon the news arrives from somewhere that he is displaying his dramatic talents with a theatrical company to the utmost delight of the people, and that the showers of favors and tokens of their appreciation visit him constantly. But the manner in which his aged parents take the affair is by itself a bit of good comedy. They bemoan themselves over their son's unsteady life, and often in their visit to us seek our condolence. Notwithstanding the apparent sorrow, whenever their boy has been heard to make a " decided hit " none are more pleased than they. The old couple, being themselves fond of gayety, extended a helping, willing hand to the dancing society wherein their son moved actively. It was, indeed, under the supervision of the good old gentleman that the huge curtain was completed; I think he designed and painted it mostly by himself.

Our young friend's presence in town naturally gave rise to a race of amateur actors. One of them particularly I recall with great interest on account of his diverse accomplishments; he tried his hand at almost every trade. I believe certain peculiarities in his childhood induced his parents to put him in a monastery. He grew up a studious boy, but indulged not infrequently in pranks. Suddenly in his early manhood it dawned upon him that he was richly endowed with the stage gift; accordingly, he left the temple behind, and, after clerking a while in his brother's store across the street from us, appeared on the stage. His versatile nature did not keep him long in that vocation; he soon sobered down to a shoemaker, discovering that the bread earned by the sweat of the brow was more to his satisfaction. That is, I concluded so in his case; he may have found, for aught I know, that by acting (such as his) he could not make a decent living and therefore had better quit playing. He was not long in making another discovery, and that was that the drudgery of the shop did not exactly suit his refined tastes. At all events, he must take a little air sometimes; he would go about the streets selling greens; yes, that was a splendid plan, combining trade and exercise. And so he turned a vegetable vender this time, nobody regarding it a too humble occupation in such a small community as ours. Later he became an amazaké man. The amazaké (sweet liquor) is prepared by subjecting soft boiled rice to saccharine fermentation and checking the process just at the point where the sugar gives up its alcohol. Hence it is sweet, palatable and very popular with children. We brewed some at home—the home-brewed! My mother had hard work to satisfy the large family of thirsty mouths.

Our man of all trades went about asking the public in all the notes of the gamut, if they would not tickle their palates with his honest "sweet liquor." To be always on foot as an itinerant tradesman, however, proved too much for his constitution. I will not take it upon me to enumerate in what other things he tried his hand; I hasten on to inform my curious reader that he shaved his head again and joined the priesthood, perfectly content with his diverse worldly experiences. In spite of his fickleness he was an honest fellow and passed for a tolerable humorist among his friends.

There was another of the number, the keeper of the tavern at the foot of a bridge that spans the little stream running through Imabari town. His figure was tall, imposing, and his expression disposed one to suspect him of a malicious, bitter character. Nature is often capricious; she was certainly capricious in this instance, for into this mould of a man she had infused a nature the most complacent and the most obliging. His comrades assigned him the part of a villain or a cruel lord. To the eye familiar with his every-day life he figured helplessly as a villain with a good heart, and seemed to spare unnecessary stabs at his victim. Yet he was scrupulously conscientious in the execution of his rôle; not a word would he omit in his speech. Once in playing a wicked lord, in order to assist the memory he copied his entire part on the face of a flat, oblong piece of wood, which he had all the time to bear erect before him as an ensign of authority. At first on the stage he was wonderfully eloquent, not a flaw occurred in his long speech. But unfortunately in the midst of an invective the sceptre slipped off his hand. His lordship's confusion was not to be described. He paused as if to give an effect of indignation, then tried to think of the rest of the harangue: it did not come. The pause was prolonged to his own uneasiness as well as to his friends. He now cast about for a decent means of taking himself off the stage. Finally with a calm, venerable, haughty air, amid giggles and suppressed laughter, my lord stalked off behind the scene.

Through these people we became acquainted with several professional players. Some people in Japan become quite enthusiastic over their favorite actors and wrestlers; they present them with beautiful posters, on which are stated their gifts, exaggerated above their actual value. These posters are pasted on all sides of the theatre or the arena for display. At the entrance to the house of amusement stands a tower, where a small drum of very high pitch is struck for some time previous to the opening of the performance. The admission to the theatre ranges from five to twenty-five sens (cents). The stage and the inside as a whole are much larger than any metropolitan or local playhouse that I have seen in America. I admit that most of our theatres are neither carpeted nor furnished with chairs, nor are they lighted with gas, nor heated. The parquet is divided into pits by bars, each admitting barely four persons in a squatting position; the bars can be removed, uniting the small pits into one large pit of any dimensions. if a party so desire. There are also what will correspond to the dress circle and the family circle. They do not protrude over the parquet, but simply line the walls like balconies. In the parquet the floor is not raised at the end farther from the stage; therefore, if Japanese ladies were to wear tall hats it would be the doomsday for gentlemen; but luckily the fair members of our community take no pride in the towering head ornaments; really they wear none. I have been speaking as if the parquet were floored; in fact, you have to sit close to the ground, mats and quilts of your own providing alone protecting you from the damp earth.

The people bring lunch with them to eat between the acts. I have the fond remembrance of my family astir over the preparation of the lunch on the day we go to see a play. We must take things we shall not be ashamed of spreading before the public; and all the more must we be careful in selecting our dishes, for not infrequently we beckon to our acquaintances in the audience to pass away with us the usual long, wearisome intervals of the Japanese theatre, during which time no music is played as in the American theatre. Of course, we must take boiled rice; it is our bread. Nobody thinks of forgetting the bread. It is not, however, carried in its bare, glutinous form; it is made into triangular, round or square masses and rolled in burned bean powder. In the collation at the theatre we dispense with the bowls and chopsticks, and use fingers in picking up the mouthfuls of rice. Of various other dishes I give up the cataloguing in despair, for my ingenious countrywomen regale us with—the Lord knows how many kinds. The delicacies are packed in several lacquered boxes, and the boxes piled one over another and wrapped in a broad piece of cloth, whose four corners are then tied on the top. When the savory burden is being carried, there usually dangles by it a gourd full of saké. The Japanese world takes no note of drinking; the saké is, moreover, mild, and, although sipped on all occasions as freely as tea, is seldom drunk to excess.

Next to the refreshment preparation is the getting ready of the girls. They spend half their life in dressing. I never was very patient; in waiting for them I was exasperated. They would lean over against the glass (or in reality a metallic mirror) in the Yum-Yum fashion for an interminable period of time, tying the girdles over fifty times before deciding upon one style, touching and retouching the coiffures, and practicing the exercise of grace. "Oh, hurry up!" I cry repeatedly in infinite chagrin, and at last become irritated beyond decency, when my mother in her persuasive, firm manner desires me to know that there is time enough. I always acquiesced in mother's decisions, because I did not like to have her call in the assistance of father. I can tell you what he would do! He would not say a word; he would curtly command me to sit beside him in the store, where people could look at me—my tears, sobs, quivering lips and all the rest of the woe. Out of shame in the exposure I would gradually compose myself, and not till I had fully recovered my temper would my father release me. I think he never struck me or my brother anywhere; the only time I saw him use force was in holding fast my little brother, who once undertook some brave proceedings against him.

The theatre usually begins late in the afternoon or early in the evening, and lasts till past midnight. In front of the stage are two large basins of vegetable oil with huge bunches of rush-wicks. They are the main sources of light; the foot-lights are a row of innumerable wax-candles; and when an actor is on the stage, men in black veils attend him with lighted candles stuck on a contrivance like a long-handled contribution box. Wherever he goes, there go with him these walking candlesticks. When he exerts himself briskly, as in a combat, with what funny jerks and fanciful motions do these mysterious lights fly round, often flickering themselves out! In the era of gas and electric light what a bungling machinery all this is!

The orchestra does not sit at the foot of the stage: it occupies a box on one side. It consists of the samisen, a big heavy bell, a drum, a flute, a conch shell and occasional singing. Over the orchestra-box is a compartment hung with a curtain woven with fine split bamboos, wherein sit two men - one with a book on a stand, the other with a stout samisen. The former explains in a harsh-voiced recital the situation of the affairs now acted before the audience, the latter keeps time with the instrument.

The dramas are mostly historical; we have no opera. In Japanese plays the passion of love takes but a subordinate rank, the paramount importance being accorded to loyalty, the spirit of retaliation and devotion to parents. Harakiri, or the cutting open of one's own abdomen in way of manly death, so time-honored and deeply believed in among the ancient samurai (soldier) class, is acted in connection with certain plays. It is an impressive, solemn scene. The valiant unfortunate stabs himself with a poniard, measuring exactly nine inches and a half, struggles with agony, shows manifold changes of expression, makes his will in a faltering voice, and leaves injunctions to the weeping relatives and faithful servants gathered round him; writhing in distress, yet undaunted in presence of cool, examining deputies, he ends his mortal life by the final act of driving the blood-stained iron into the throat.

One strange fact respecting the theatrical profession in our country is the anomaly that men act women's parts. We have few or no actresses. The taste of the people took a curious turn in its development; they consider those actors perfect who can deceive them most dexterously in female outfits. Acting has been from ages past regarded as a profession exclusively for men; their wives travel with them as a sort of slave in assisting their masters and husbands in painting and dressing behind the scene. Therefore, once when a company of women went about giving entertainments there was a considerable stir over the novelty; they soon became known as the "female theatre." In this party there were few or no men, the women assuming male characters. These actresses established fame on their wonderfully natural delineations of masculine traits.

We have known a young actor, whose boyhood was spent in Imabari, make a mark in representing female characters. He copied the grace and deportment of the fair sex archly. We took great interest in him, for he was a good, quiet, sensible fellow, and his parents had formerly dwelt near and befriended us. But my friends were wont to comment that his neck was a jot too full for that of a female. He could not help that; the corpulency of that member was a freak of nature; he was not at all responsible for it. Discreetly he tried none of your fooleries with dieting to reduce it; some females, you know, are not very slender-necked either; he might have taken comfort in that. At any rate, his manners were thoroughly feminine, and his womanly way of speaking a woman herself could not imitate. Our friend is now gone to a metropolis, where he is winning his way into the hearts of the millions. Prosperity and success to his name!

When the "female theatre" troupe was in Imabari, through somebody's introduction we got acquainted with certain of their number. We asked them to call at our house. They did so. We observed no trace of forwardness in them; instead, they, all of them, seemed quite reticent. I remember a dear little creature, Kosei (Little Purity) by name, among them. She was perfectly at ease in playing a rollicking little rogue before the crowd, but now hung her head timidly and lifted stealthily her big round eyes to us. She had a sweet, pretty little mouth. Where can that poor, mischievous, pretty waif be knocking about in the wide world now-a-days? Perhaps she is grown up and uninteresting, if yet living.

I can recall even what we gave them that evening with which to refresh themselves. We ordered the zenzai or its ally, the shiruko, at the establishment round the corner. The shiruko seems like hot, thick chocolate, with bits of toast in it. The chocolate part is prepared of red beans, and the toast is the browned mochi (rice-cake). To provide for any among them that did not love sweet things we had the soba or the udon brought to us by their vender. The soba is a sort of vermicelli made of buckwheat, and the udon a kind of macaroni, solid and not in tubes. The warm katsuwo sauce is plentifully poured over them, and they are eaten with chopsticks. The katsuwo sauce is prepared of the katsuwobushi and the shoyu. The first named article is a hard substance shaped somewhat like the horn of an ox, and manufactured of the flesh of certain fish, whose vernacular name is katsuwo. A family cannot get along without it. In preparing the sauce, the katsuwobushi is simply chipped and simmered in a mixture of water and the shoyu. The shoyu is a sauce by itself and brewed of wheat, beans and salt. As its use in domestic cookery is very wide, the demand for it is correspondingly great; and the shoyu brewing is as big a business as the saké manufacturing.

## CHAPTER VII.

Our family cared but little for the wrestling exhibition; some people have a great liking for it. It takes place on an extensive open lot. In the middle of the field is raised a large, square mound, from the corners of which rise four posts decorated with red and white cloths, looking like a barber's sign. They support an awning. The spectators, too, are shielded from the sun with cheap mats strapped together. On the mound is described a circle, within which the matches take place. The two opposite parties are called East and West respectively. The umpire in kamishimo (ceremonial garb) calls out a champion from each side by his professional name so loudly as to be heard all over the place. The names are derived from the mighty objects in nature, such as mountain, river, ocean, storm, wind, thunder, lightning, forest, crag, etc. The two naked, gigantic, muscular fellows slowly ascend the arena, drink a little water from ladles, take pinches of common salt from small baskets hanging on two of the posts and, looking up reverently to a paper god fastened to the awning, throw the salt around. It is an act of purification, and while doing it each prays secretly for his own success. Then they stamp heavily on the ground, with their hands on their bent knees and their hips lowered, in order to get the muscles ready for action. Now they face each other in a low sitting posture like that of a frog; at the word of signal from the umpire they instantly spring up, and each tries to throw the other or push him out of the circular arena. There are many professional tricks that they deal out in the struggle for supremacy. As soon as the point is decided the umpire indicates the victor's side with his Chinese fan. Then follows the demonstration of joy among the patrons of the successful almost as boisterous and enthusiastic as that of the young American collegians at their grand athletic contests. The thousands sitting hitherto well behaved on the matted ground rise up at once and make endless tumult; cups, bottles, empty lacquered boxes fly into the arena from every direction. Not infrequently a spirited controversy follows a questionable decision of the umpire. Between the matches gifts from the patrons are publicly announced and sometimes displayed.

The people sit on the ground, spread with mats, in the open air, and eat and drink, while they watch the collision of the two mountains of flesh and its momentous issue. The exhibition cannot very well take place on rainy days. At the end of a day's performance, all the wrestlers in gorgeous aprons march to the arena as the umpire claps two blocks of hard wood, and go through a simple ceremony of stretching the arms in various directions formally. I never inquired what it was for, my childish fancy having been turned toward the aprons, which were oriental gold embroidery-work in relief on velvet, plush and other kinds of cloth. On the way home the spectators notice on the fences the announcement of the matches for the morrow. At the close of a series of the contests, which continue about three days, the favorite wrestlers go the round of their patrons in fine silk garments.

We were fond of listening to story-tellers. The entertainment takes place at night in a public hall. A company of story-tellers travel together under the name of their leader. In the early part of the evening the unskillful members come out in turn, and serve to kill time and practice on the audience. On the platform there is nothing to be seen but a low table and a candle burning on each side of it. A narrator appears from behind the curtain on the back of the platform, and sits at the table on a cushion and makes a profound bow. Then he takes a sip of tea, stops the samisen playing by banging upon the table with two fans wrapped in leather; he murmurs a courteous welcome to the audience, bows repeatedly, and, after snuffing the candles, proceeds with a story. The stories are chiefly humorous or witty until toward the end of the evening, when the abler men make their appearance and the tenor of the narrative insensibly takes on a serious aspect and a tragic interest. The comic stories invariably terminate with sprightly puns, the tragic in a spectacular representation of ghosts and spirits. An awful tale of murder, let us suppose, has been told in an impressive manner; and while the imaginary murderer and the actual listeners are seeing strange sights in fancy, the narrator unobserved turns down the lights and tumbles off the platform. In the following darkness the ghosts stalk in a ray of pale light; they are the story-tellers themselves in masks, and they sometimes walk down the aisles to the terror of those that believe in them. I could not bear the roving apparitions,—I was small indeed,—and took refuge in the lap of my elder companion, much as certain birds hide their heads, and think themselves safe. No doubt such sights as these worked in my infant imagination, and roused in me that dread of darkness which is so common with the children of Japan.

On fine days in spring our neighborhood went out *en masse* on excursion parties. They roamed about the warm green fields at will and gathered in hand-baskets, half dallying with the sunbeams, various kinds of wild herbs which are tender and edible, or they feasted in a charming nook underneath the canopy of cherry blossoms. The pink petals of the full blown flowers, fanned by a gentle breath of wind, visited the merry-makers like snow-flakes; a single flake occasionally happening to fall in the tiny earthen cup of saké, held up by one who stopped and talked or laughed just as he was putting it to his lips. The party was wonderfully pleased at that; if they were a poetical club or artistic coterie such little accidents perhaps elicited short rhythmical effusions from them, which they would pen on beautiful variegated cards expressly cut for the purpose. These would be tied to the drooping branches, that the next party might pause to share in the sentiment of the present instance. More frequently, however, this is done to leave some token of the culture and refinement of the clique, or to show off the individual's finish of hand and elegance of expression. Vanity is at the bottom of it.

We sat on the scarlet Chinese blanket, spread on the greensward; wine made every heart buoyant; the happy crew, by and by, sang, played the samisen and tripped "the light fantastic toe." Indeed, nothing could call us home, after such enjoyment of a beautiful day, but the reddening western sky and the falling shades of night.

At Imabari we have an excellent public garden in the ruins of the old castle. In spring when all the cherry trees bloom in full force, the scene, surveyed at a distance, looks like the piles of white cloud in the blue summer sky. You must know the Japanese cultivate the cherry-tree not for its fruit, but for the beauty of its flowers. If the tree bears fruit, it is bitter to the taste, worse than your choke-cherries; nobody stops to pluck it. When past the height of blooming, the flowers begin to leave the boughs quietly; later they fall abundantly and quickly, and, alighting on the dirt below, cover it like a sheet of snow. Trite as this description may appear, it has yet a charm for me; for the happy time I spent under those blossoms, in that mellow sun and that soft open air, steals back imperceptibly in my memory.

In the centre of the garden stands a shrine of the Shinto gods. The entire ground is considerably elevated above the level of the surrounding regions, and stone walls hem it in. A belt of deep ditches, which, in the warlike days of old, stemmed the rush of an invading army, girdles the base of the steep walls. The neglect of years, passed in peace, has left it in disrepair. To some of the trenches the ebb and flow of sea-water have still access, and swarms of big fish and little fish thrive unmolested, for none but the people that pay for the privilege are permitted to angle in these fish-ponds. There are also fresh-water moats; the beds of green pond-weeds and duck's meat closely patch the sluggish, dark-colored waters. Here grows the famous lotus plant of the East. It shoots up its broad umbrella-like leaves in summer, and on the stalks here and there among the leaves open the Buddhist's pure majestic flowers.

Having heard that the buds unlock in an instant at early dawn with the noise of percussion, we, the curious, formed a little party for the purpose of investigating the truth of it. We arose a little after midnight, gathered together the pledged and groped our way in the dark; we could scarcely discern one another. By the time, however, we arrived at our destination, it was close upon daybreak; a party at the further end of the bank showed darkly against the aurora of the eastern sky, for the country round was open and nothing stood between us and the sea. We kept vigil intently; for my part I failed to observe any of the buds open; having watched a great many at the same time I really watched none. A clever person instructed me that my whole attention should be paid to a single bud; for which reason I the next time pitched upon one particular bud. I kept my eye on it all the morning, looking neither to the right nor to the left. I was once before provoked at a spiral bud of morning-glory in my garden, because it intentionally unfurled upon me when I was looking aside. Accordingly, I took especial care against such failure on my part; but it all proved vain—the lotus bud was too young to blossom!

The flowers are very large; white is the common color, but then there is a rare lovely pink shade. The plant bears edible fruit; the root, too, is counted a delicacy. By reason of the unknown depth of the black mud, wherein the roots lie hidden, the plucking of them is very difficult; the men formerly held in contempt under the name of Etta dive in the mire and search for them. The prized article is seen, immersed in water, in grocery stores on sale; no feast of any pretension is complete without it. When sliced crosswise the renkon (lotus root) shows about half-a-dozen symmetrical holes; the slices are boiled with the katsuwo and shoyu and are valued highly for toothsomeness.

Some of the wide ditches were filled up from time to time; and in the places where fishes had frisked about or warriors tried to float a raft, farmers were now peacefully hoeing potatoes, or pumpkins basked their heads in the noontide sun. But the castle, being too colossal to be pulled down at once, remained entire for a long time, after the feudal system had been abolished and the Lord of Imabari summoned to Yedo. Unfortunately, however, the extensive underground powder magazine one morning caught a spark of fire, and all of a sudden the towers and palaces blew up with a tremendous explosion. At that period the Japanese apprehended the possible invasion of the "red-haired devils," the foreigners; for which reason it was not to be wondered at that the patriotic citizens of Imabari mistook the earth-rending roar and the heavy ascending columns of smoke in the direction of the old stronghold for a cannonade of enemies. The panic it produced in town struck terror into everybody's heart; the weak and nervous fell into fits. A drizzling rain since the previous eve rendered the streets excessively wet. Splashing in the mud and puddles, the heroic of the townsmen, with the loose dangling skirt of the Japanese garment tucked up through the belt for action, hurried castleward with the utmost speed, with unsheathed spear and sword in hand, to the great consternation of the astounded populace. I was scarcely of an age to comprehend the dire calamity, yet the scene impressed me indelibly. Soon the vision of foreign hairy invaders vanished; the people saw that it was a sheer accident, fearful as it was; but in that ancient lax administration behind the screen of cruel rigidity, the real cause of it has never been thoroughly investigated. Lives were lost in the disaster, for a multitude of servants still lived in the castle. Mutilated limbs and bodies were subsequently picked up in abundance from the surrounding moats; the features of many were too badly marred for identification; and as to the severed limbs no one could tell which belonged to which of the shattered trunks.

The remaining half-burned buildings have since been destroyed piecemeal; all that now remains of the proud castle is the innermost circle of masonry, which cannot so easily be leveled to the ground. It is not provided with a railing, and in looking down the steep one feels his heart stand still. The vast prospect it commands, extending far beyond the town limits, is superb. A man taking the path directly below the wall appears no bigger than a dot.

Since I have begun a long story about this grand ruin, give me leave to recount a tradition in connection with it. Back in the dark ages the superstitious belief existed in Japan, that in building a castle, to secure the firmness of its foundation a human life should be sacrificed. Usually a person was buried alive beneath one of the walls; some declare the efficacy nullified unless the victim be taken in unawares. The chronicle says, that in conformity to the above belief when the Imabari castle, was being raised a horrible homicide had been committed. At first the authorities were much at a loss in the choice of a proper offering. One day a poor, decrepit old woman, either prompted by curiosity or to beg money of the men, approached the work; little did she dream her life was in peril; in an instant a sagacious magistrate solved the problem. The signal nod from him, and the castle-builders fell upon the crone and, amid her screams, struggles, entreaties, stoned her to the earth. Henceforward, it is said, in the dead silence of the castle at night a faint, pitiful cry, now drowned in the soughing storm outside, now audible in the dreadful pause, echoes from under the ground. I had the precise spot pointed out to me; it lies in the centre of all the outlying bulwarks; in passing it I always felt a thrill steal through me, and turned that corner at a greater angle than I would an ordinary corner, with the intention of keeping my feet off the buried bones.

In those tyrannical days of feudalism the samurais presumed much upon the commoners of the town. They not only laid claim wrongly to their personal property, but also regarded their lives as of no importance. The samurai always carried two swords by his side, one long and one short, to arbitrate right and wrong in altercations. Blades tempered by certain smiths were particularly esteemed; and in order to test the cutting edge, he would lie in wait nightly at a street corner for a victim. An innocent passer-by was ferociously attacked and, unless he could defend himself, was wantonly slain. Such outrages actually occurred in places; people, forthwith, seldom stirred abroad nights. Heaven be thanked, those savage times are gone forever; the street-lamps light every nook and corner, and the police guard the safety of the citizen.

## CHAPTER VIII.

My mother is fond of parties and young people and their keen appreciation of pleasure; my father is of a far different turn of mind; he has his happiest moments in smoking leisurely, in manipulating the fishing-rod and line, under the shielding pine-tree, by some quiet river-bank, or in hunting out edible mushrooms in the mountains. He is a respectable, practical Izaak Walton; quaint ripples of smile pass across his face as the nibbling fish gives his line a tantalizing pull; he helps me bait, he teaches me when and how to make sure of my spoil,—for many a victim hangs to the hook just long enough to rise out of water, glitters transiently in the sun and thrills one with joy, and then decides, undeceived, to reject the dainty morsel: there rises an ever widening, ever receding circle on the still liquid surface, a golden flap of the tail, and the fish is invisible, leaving one despondent. I liked mother's and sisters' company, but also appreciated father's soothing, restful influence. At the simple repast in the open solitary scene of the field and stream, after angling all the morning, he said little; yet the expression of calm enjoyment and honest humor on his face brightened his companion. Those were delightful times; I have the scene at this moment before my mental eye:—the broad beach of white sand surrounding the cove, where the river meets the sea, with a lonely stork standing on one leg in shallow water; the briny odor from the sea, and the fresh scent from the meadow; the sighing pines overhead and the turbulent water at the stone abutments of the bridge; the sunny blue sea beyond the sand-bar, studded with white sails; a huge cloud of smoke swaying landward, rising from the distant brick-yard; and in the grayish-blue background the silhouette of a grove and knoll, whereon a wayside shrine stands.

"See what you can do about here," says my father, taking in his line, "I shall follow the river up and find if they bite." He turns his back and disappears and reappears among the scrub oaks and stunted willows that fringe the margin. I stay where I am like a good son; but being no more successful than before, and bored and wishing company, after a reasonable lapse of time, I find myself going after my father. Upon finding him quietly seated under some protruding tree, beneath whose mirrored branches and near whose knotty root the water darkens in a pool, I inquire into his success. "No, nothing marvelous," he responds gently, gazing dreamily across the river, yet wary with the fish that "cometh as a thief in the night." I take the liberty of lifting the lid of his basket and peep at the contents; a large trout disturbed by the jar I gave it, snaps violently—I let down the lid instantly at that--and then it lies exhausted, working its jaw in anguish for water.

"Cast your fly and try your luck," says my excellent father. Of course I obey him; and although I was not so successful every time as he, yet could not always help observing privately that the location he had selected was a good fishing hole.

The river I have in mind has a characteristic oriental appellation given it—Dragon-fire. It is a small stream at a short distance from the town of Imabari, having its fountain-heads in the valleys of the mountains visible from the mouth. There is nothing remarkable about this water-course, except a popular belief that, on the eve of a festal day in honor of the temple situated on one of the mountains, a mysterious fire rises from the enchanting "dragon-palace" in the depths of the ocean, where a beautiful queen reigns supreme over her charming watery world with its finny and scaly subjects of various species. The mysterious light, casting an inverted image on the water, moves steadily up the river, under the concentrated gaze of thousands who climb the height partly as devotees but mostly as spectators, until it reaches a massive stone lantern erected upon the ledge of an immense cliff. There it vanishes as strangely as it appeared; and instead the lantern, hitherto dark, lights up suddenly.

I dislike to question the reality of this astonishing phenomenon, or try to explain it with my superficial knowledge of physics. A very pious, gracious old lady in our neighborhood had always a ready listener in me in her superstitious talks concerning the wonders and charitable doings of the Goddess of Mercy, whom she had imposingly enshrined in her apartment and adored unceasingly. Perhaps you would wish to know what the goddess looked like. Well, it was a small bronze statuette in a gilded miniature temple; she wore a scanty Hindoo costume, a halo around her head and an expression gentle, sweet, serene, godly.— You have seen a reproduction of the ideal Italian picture of Christ, with downcast eyes and a look of meek submission, benign tenderness and forgiveness: the Goddess of Mercy seemed quite like that but with slightly more authority. Another conception of the pagan goddess, which I have seen elsewhere, represents her as possessing countless arms, signifying, I imagine, the countless deeds of mercy she achieves for mankind.

The good old lady did not feel satisfied with the home worship; she must play the pilgrim, in spite of years and infirmities, and visit, at least, the nearest public temples. So she set off with her company, a circle of aged zealots like herself, on a journey to a sacred edifice standing somewhere in the mountain which, in fair weather, shows faintly against the sky west of Imabari, towering far above hills and heights of nearer distances. The way is long and tedious and lies through rocky regions. Difficult passes and precipitous declivities were left far behind by assiduous traveling on foot; but the party lost the way, wandered into mountain wilds, silent and sublime, far, far from home or any human habitation; and there was nothing to be heard but the flocks of rooks cawing inauspiciously among the tree-tops. The day advanced rapidly; the sun wheeled down without tarrying, and in the trackless forest the evening gloom gathered early. Mute admiration, commingled with despair, seized the travelers as they surveyed the forest grandeur in its twilight robe. The unpruned trees thrust out dry broken arms from near the roots; the leaves sere and sodden covered the damp, black soil ankle deep rustling under the tread.

The sunset, how glorious! Our travelers threw down their walking-sticks, stretched out their tired limbs and, seated on rocks, spell-bound, gave themselves up to the contemplation of the magnificent fire-painting in the western firmament. Behold the mountains of living coal, the lakes of molten gold, the islands of floating amber, all irregularly shaped as by a wild genius, distributed not as on the earth's surface,—a mountainous pile super-imposed on a lake with a stratum of sapphire between! At length, the whole melted into one grand universal conflagration; the undulating tops of the distant mountain-chain appeared boldly against the horizon; the needles and cones of a pine branch, pendant near by in the line of vision, depicted themselves sharply on the canvas of crimson splendor.

Insensibly to our musing friends, however, the red sinking disc finally departed by the western portal, the after-glow died away slowly; and when they awoke from reveries and heaved a sigh, the question of what to be done came pressing upon them. Now the day being over, there was the danger of wild animals in the woods. That could be averted by building a bright fire, but what was to be done for hunger which began to assert itself strongly? With energy gone and darkness and peril thickening about them, yet trusting in the Goddess, the lonely pilgrims peered around for a less exposed spot to nestle in. In this their search, miraculously they came upon what to them looked like a cottage. It was one of the hovels hastily put up with twigs and shrubs by hunters, where they waylay the boar at night and in snow, and where they slice meat, lie by the fire and smoke, and frequently hold a midnight revel over their fat game. Our weary, almost famished tourists entered it, wondering and looking around at each step; they were at once struck with the snug appearance of the interior. There was a heap of ashes, which when disturbed disclosed a few glowing embers; and in a corner was piled on raw hide plenty of excellent venison. The hunters must have left not long since.

The pious old lady goes on to tell that such a thing as this could not have been otherwise than by the dispensation of her merciful Goddess, and that she and her fellow believers fell immediately on their knees to express their heart-felt gratitude for her munificence and protection. The fire was rekindled and fed with armfuls of the dried leaves and dead branches that lay strewn plentifully around; the broad blaze cast an illusive cheerfulness on objects standing near; each time a stick was thrown in the cloven tongues of the fire emitted sparks, which died in their flight among the masses of the overhanging foliage. Taken in connection with the surrounding scene, there was something inexpressibly wild and primitive about the open fire. The party appeased their hunger and waited the return of the proprietors of the rude cottage. They did not come, though the night advanced far; some of the pilgrims were extremely fatigued and dropped to sleep in the warmth, others sat up resolutely, repeating prayers and counting the beads before a pocket image of the Goddess. The low night wind bore to their ear, at intervals, the concert of wolves howling in dismal, forlorn cadence; and they were now and then started by one of these savage marauders appearing in their sight at a safe distance.

The night was passed in this way, and the dawn came; but how to find the right path? While they were in despair and supplicating aid from the Goddess, one of them descried a figure on the brow of an eminence not far distant. It seemed, on nearer approach, to be a venerable mountain sire; his long silver-white beard flowed down his breast; a pair of clear beaming eyes twinkled beneath his great shaggy eyebrows. Being asked in which point of the compass lay the road to the temple, he slowly lifted his cane, a knotty stem of a shrub called akaza, and indicated the west. Apropos of this, the akaza stick is believed to be carried by an imaginary race of men hidden in China's pathless woods and mountains, who are without exception very old but never overtaken by disease or death and live in serene felicity, gathering medicinal herbs, writing on scrolls and in company with cranes and tortoises. In kakemonoes (wall hangings) they are sometimes depicted as taking a literal " flying " visit on craneback, with the inevitable scroll in hand, to their brother sennin's (sennin is the name this happy race goes by) grotto in a neighboring hill or dale.

Our party of wanderers thanked the kind but dignified old man on their hands and knees and raised their heads, when he seemed to dissolve away from view in a most singular manner. This opportune guide, according to my garrulous lady, is a messenger sent by her thousand-armed Goddess to their help; in fine, not a thing occurs but is ordained by Kwannon the Merciful. The story of the adventure was wound up with the safe arrival in the Kwannon temple, and fervent piety kindled at the altar.

## CHAPTER IX.

I AM afraid I have told a long prosaic story in the previous chapter, and betrayed a school-boy-like delight for the bombastic in the description of the sunset, etc. No one detests more than I any thing that smacks of the young misses' poetry. Come, let us inquire, more relevantly to our purpose, what constituted my childish happiness, sorrow, fear and other kindred feelings in Japan.

The greatest fear I can yet recall was the ordeal of the yaito. This is a Japanese domestic art of healing and averting diseases, especially those of children. The moxa, being made into numerous tiny cones and placed on certain spots on the back, is lighted with the senko already described. Imagine how you feel when the flesh is being burnt; I used to hold out stoutly against the cruel operation—would you not sympathize with me? If I had any presentiment of it, I would slip away and keep from home till I became desirous of dinner. No sooner had I crossed the paternal threshold than I was made a prisoner; and ailment or no ailment, my severe father and mother insisted upon my having the yaito once in so often. Great was my demonstration of agony when father held me still and mother proceeded to burn my bare back; a promise of bonbons, which reconciled me to almost anything ordinarily, did not work in this one instance; I cried myself hoarse (keeping it up even while there was no pain) and kicked frantically. "The storm is over," mother used to say with considerable relief, when the trial drew to a close; she hated the torture as much as anybody, but she had the welfare of her child at heart. Ah, gentle mother, if I had only understood you then as I do now I should certainly not have snapped so terribly. I remember, after twenty-four to forty-eight hours the blisters began to swell and chafed painfully against the clothing, and had to be punctured to let out the serum. As a matter of fact, the yaito did cure slight general and local ailments: once I had a blood-shot eye, and mother sent me to a worthy old woman in town who knew how to cure it by means of yaito. After much pressing with fingers, she hit at the vital point in the back and marked it with a generous dip of india ink. Upon returning home, it was burnt deeply with moxa; and miraculously enough the eye got well immediately. I am inclined to think the cautery acts through the nerves. Now for years have I been exempt from the operation, yet to this day on my back are symmetrically branded the star-like memorials of my mother's love.

Speaking of the old woman I am reminded of another whom I was in the habit of looking upon as a sort of witch. Her eye, with the crow's foot at the outer corner and, I fancied, with the pupil in a longitudinal slit like that of grimalkin, the creature nearest to witches and warlocks; her fetich, the image of a human monkey, to whom she was a sort of vestal virgin; her place of abode remote from town and isolated from other farm-houses, presenting a queer combination of a rustic home and a sacred shrine; these made my childish imagination invest her with an air of mystery. She was wont to come to town in trim, made-over clothes re-dyed and starched, with the slant overlapping Japanese collars adjusted nicely; in the setta (slipper-sandals, much liked by aged people for their ease and safety compared with the high clogs); with her gray-streaked black hair combed tightly up, glossy with a superabundance of pomatum and done up in a coiffure bespeaking her age; walking firmly, with a small portable shrine on her back wrapt in the furoshiki (wide cloth for carrying things about) and tied around her shoulders. People sent for her to exorcise their houses, particularly when there happened to be sick persons in them, consulted her in selecting the site for a new building and in sinking the well, in order not to draw upon their heads the vengeance of a displeased spirit. On some occasions our household required her assistance; I went the long distance through the open fields to her residence; and when she came she let down the shrine from her back, placed it against the wall in our sitting-room and, opening reverentially the hinge-doors, proceeded to pray. What for, I don't remember, I was too intent upon her manners to inquire into her purpose.

Of quite another stamp was Aunt Otsuné (so everybody called her), housekeeper to the prosperous candy dealer just opposite us on Main street.

Ready with tears for any sad news; sympathetic in the extreme; beaming, radiant, full of happy smiles in beholding her friends—methinks I see her snatch me from my nurse's arms, fondle me to her bosom and press her withered cheek against my fat one, uttering some such very encouraging ejaculation as "My precious dear!" She did not kiss me, I am very certain, for we don't have kissing. And she must have many a time dropped her work to admire my holiday garment; I know I toddled some of my early experimental steps in journeys to Aunty, trailing behind me the free ends of my sash; and as I became confident of myself, I became ambitious and dragged my father's or brother's clogs, a world too big for my feet. O how good Aunty was! She would fill both my hands with the candies that were being prepared in the back of the store near the kitchen and bid me run home and show them to mamma. The best thing she was in the habit of bestowing upon me was —I don't know what to call it; it was the burnt bottom portion of the rice she had cooked for all hands of the store in a prodigious vessel, loosened in broad pieces and folded about the an. The an is (this necessity of definition upon definition cautions me against touching on many a thing peculiarly Japanese) the an is a red bean deprived of its skin and mashed with sugar; it forms the core of various comfits. O how I relished this Aunty's homely, warm, sweet concoction! It was not intended for sale, therefore we cared little about its appearance, were it only good to taste. She made it so large sometimes that I had to hold it with both my small hands. I munched away at it, whilst she scraped the great vessel; and it was sometime before each of us could finish our huge tasks. I well recall the flickering rush-light under which Aunty worked: the sense of satisfaction I experienced in my agreeable occupation in my corner; the harsh grating noise of the steel scraper against the bottom of the iron vessel; the obscurity round about the sink a short way off; and the invisible rascals of mice holding high festivity over cast-off viands, chasing each other, biting one another's tails and screeching at the pain. My family endeavored to keep me at home, for it certainly is not in good taste to have one's child running off to a neighbor's kitchen; but Aunty would steal me from mamma, and I, for my part, did all I could, I warrant, to be stolen!

When we are well-nigh through our business, Aunty, happening to glance at me to assure herself I am there though silent, breaks into a broad, good-humored smile at the sight. Here I am with the an smeared about my mouth, and stretching out my hands equally sticky, in a most comic despairing attitude. What I implore in mute eloquence is this, that she would please to take immediate care of my soiled hands and wipe off the material about my mouth. Aunty stands a minute appreciating the humorous effect so produced; I look up at her with unsuspecting eyes wide open and licking my mouth occasionally by way of variation. Soon, however, my good-hearted Aunty washes me nice and clean and taking me up with her hands on my sides, throws me on her right shoulder and crosses over to the opposite side of the street in short quick steps to our house. She is always a welcome guest there and is at once surrounded by our women, to whom she imparts her kitchen lore and latest bits of news about men and things.

She had a little romance in her kitchen, which she helped along and she took absorbing interest in its development. It was the mutual attachment of the adopted daughter of the great candy manufacturer and one of his men. Miss Chrysanthemum, to give a glimpse of her past history, was born in a humble home and, being a burden to its inmates, was thrust upon Mr. Gladness the Main street confectioner, who was immensely wealthy, and invested for pleasure in peacocks, canary birds, white, long-eared, pink-eyed, lovely, tame rabbits, valuable pot-plants and many other good things. I received beautiful peacock feathers from him; but my sisters did not wish them for their bonnets, because Japanese ladies do not wear bonnets. (But I don't know, of course, as I am a man and a foreigner, that ladies ever trim their bonnets with the gay peacock feathers.) And when the peacocks died, Mr. Gladness (his Japanese equivalent means it) caused them to be stuffed and surprised me and many others one day with the dead but life-like peacocks in the cage. I went to see Mr. Gladness often; Mr. Gladness was a very rich, important gentleman; Mr. Gladness was good enough to me, though older people did not seem to love him as I did; he let me see the rabbits eat bamboo-leaves. He said I might touch them if I liked. I was very much afraid at first, but Mr. Gladness assured me they wouldn't bite—honestly they wouldn't. So I ventured to put out my hand. They limped away from me though, keeping their noses going all the time. Don't you know how they twitch their noses? Japanese rabbits do that too; I thought it was funny! Mr. Gladness had in his yard a large pond, where he kept a lot of big goldfish; Mr. Gladness had also in his beautiful yard a little mountain and a little stream with a little bridge. Mr. Gladness had a great many servants; everybody, bowing, said "yea, yea" to him, while he stood straight as an arrow.

Miss Chrysanthemum, as I was saying, came, or rather was brought to this rich merchant's house, he having found her one cold morning at his door, tucked nicely in a basket, like little Moses. Her poor dear mother, like his mother, some have said, was watching from a hiding place; the anxiety of a mother seems the same both in ancient and modern times and all the world over. Now the rich man had no child, just as in stories; and when the crying baby stopped and smiled at him through her tears, his proud old heart felt infinitely tender. He adopted her at that instant and christened her afterward Chrysanthemum, the flower of that name being his favorite above all others in his garden.

These particulars I gleaned from the neighbors' social gossip after I had grown up; Miss Chrysanthemum was already a young lady when I used to go to Aunt Otsuné in childish adoration. I remember the young lady took me one winter's evening beside her to the kotatsu, the heating apparatus I have mentioned in connection with my grandfather's house, and told me stories. She was reared in luxury, had everything she wanted that could be gotten with money, and was a great pet of Aunty's, who regarded her as her own child. It was not surprising, then, that Aunty should note with deep satisfaction the gentle flutter of Miss Chrysanthemum's maiden heart at the sight of a young man; indeed, she seemed in the eye of the world to take more interest than the interested parties themselves. This kitchen romance was the pervading theme of her conversation; we were in duty bound to hear just how the matter stood between the two, with her opinions as to the prospect. The whole town took it up and discussed it variously; some sage persons shook their heads and intimated that they knew a certain poor fisherwoman to be Miss Chrysanthemum's real mother, and that they had all along their own misgivings concerning the young lady's future. "The blood will tell" was the maxim on which these sapient observers took their stand, and they talked the young man over as if he were an arrant fortune hunter, when I fear not one of them could come up to Mr. Prosperity in assiduity and honest labor. "The blood will tell," indeed, that a daughter of a friendless, mistaken, but upright woman should choose for herself a sensible man, one who will stick to her through thick and thin, as we shall see presently.

As I am not writing a love story, I shall not give the personal appearances of my fair Chrysanthemum and gentle Prosperity, nor their sayings and doings. Yet I do see perfectly, even at this distance of time and place, the picture of young Mr. Prosperity sitting with his fellow workers at his work, in the workshop on the rear of the store, under the same roof with the kitchen but with a hall-way between. Perhaps he is putting a color on the sugared commodities; he does it with a flat brush, taking up the pieces one by one, then he sends a box of them to the next man, who goes over the same, staining the uncolored portion with another tint. He looks up at my approach, smiles a welcome and resumes the work; the others, being used to my coming, go on with their job, without even taking as much trouble as the mere act of raising their heads, saying indifferently "halloo!" to their busy hands. Mr. Prosperity, I remember, gave me some of the candy he was making when he found an opportunity, which went farther to form my good opinion of him than any other act.

Everything went on pleasantly with the young people and Aunty—very pleasantly, in fact, until the pleasure of the old gentleman came to be consulted. Then arose an insurmountable difficulty: he would not hear of the match; he possessed wealth and in consequence proved supercilious. His wealth, however, was but recently acquired; he himself was once a common workman in a candy store on the fourth block of the same street. But he would not have anything said about it; he simply would not brook the idea of giving his daughter in marriage to his employee; he foolishly deemed it below his dignity. This was a severe blow to Aunt Otsuné; she felt her career balked and frustrated; the young couple began to love each other much more than before. "What would this state of things result in?" said the gossips of the town. Reconciliation of the huffy old man, impossible! Separation of the affectionate pair, quite as hard!

Here Aunt Otsuné called in her inventive powers; she was full of kind honest invention,—how else could she have carried herself in the battle of life so far, single handed, and remain a favorite with all the world? She took Miss Chrysanthemum and Mr. Prosperity under her wing, as it were, rented a comfortable little house on a by-street and installed them therein, married. She liked to see them happy together, and have them take care of her in her old age; she had heretofore been lone and helpless, despite her cheerful exertions. They opened a small candy store, falling back upon their knowledge of the trade; soon there came to them a dear little babe. Aunt Otsuné rejoiced at the little one's advent; her scheme was now complete. She bore the infant in her arms softly and went to the door of her former employer. Her diplomacy was to give the cross old fellow a sight of the lovely grandchild and thereby work a miracle in his stony heart, surmising at the same time that time must have done something towards mollifying his obstinacy. This accomplished, it would be an easy step to persuade him to take them all back into his favor. Alas, poor faithful soul! it was but a woman's wisdom: Mr. Gladness was still found inexorable.

On that memorable night slowly she walked into our house with the babe in her arms, and sat herself down heavily by the dim, papered Japanese household lamp. For some time she remained silent and glanced around the room furtively; to her unspeakable satisfaction there was nobody there beside ourselves. Then the mental tension with which she upheld the whole weight of misery and woe gave way, and she burst into a flood of tears. I recollect the unusual solemn hush of the room, the serious looks of the company and the distracting sobs on the other side of the lamp; I recollect my becoming unaccountably sad, too, and looking away at a corner in my effort to refrain from tears; I beheld the paper god pasted high up on the pillar brown with age and smoke. When Aunty recovered herself, she managed to inform us how she had been received by Mr. Gladness and told us she had made up her mind, if the young people were willing, to move to one of the islands in the Sound where she was sure of a kindlier reception. So the kind old soul, foiled in the last of her struggles, left her friends at Imabari for the simple life of the islanders. At intervals, we had intelligence of her whereabouts, but as years rolled on news reached us no more.

I have given this account of Aunt Otsuné somewhat at length, because I felt interested in reviving her half-forgotten memory; and I have entered upon the history of Miss Chrysanthemum and Mr. Prosperity in order to show to the people of this country, who are misinformed on the subject of Japanese marriage and believe that our young people are, in all cases, matched by their parents and not infrequently to those whom they do not love,— in order to show, I say, to these misinformed people by an actual example from my own observation, that such is not the case, and that our people marry for love of each other, notwithstanding the artificial manners of our society.

## CHAPTER X.

I WAS generally happy in my childish days in Japan. I cannot put my finger on any particular thing as my chief happiness, but I think holidays made me as happy as anything. We have a number of holidays, among which the first and the greatest is New Year's Day.

The first three days of January! I shall never forget them. But like most celebrations New Year pleasure must be chiefly felt in a few preparatory days. In Japan full vigor is preserved among children for Happy New Year; here in America Merry Christmas, with its Santa Claus and his stockingful of presents, takes away the zest from children before New Year comes. The merriment of the season is materially heightened by the making of the mochi. The mochi, which I have referred to once before, is a glutinous cake made of rice; it is as peculiarly indispensable in the New Year feast as is turkey in the New England Thanksgiving dinner. It is generally no larger than a man's palm, therefore one family makes a great number of them. Many are stuffed with the an. The an is not necessarily sweet; some people like it flavored with salt. A large number of the mochis are not stuffed; they are suffered to dry and harden, so that they can be stored away for future enjoyment. At any time during the year you may get them out and steam or toast them. In our town there are men who make it their business to visit houses and help them in mochi-making. Just before New Year the professional mochi-makers work hard day after day. They could not always come in the daytime and made arrangements to visit us in the early morning. Then my sisters and I could hardly go to sleep in the great anticipation of joy. When the morning came, our house was thrown open, illuminated (for it was yet dark) brightly and cheerfully, and the whole household were up doing something with willing hand and heart. I cannot describe how happy I was in this scene. I tried, half in play, to help them and got in everybody's way. You know the holiday feelings are very difficult to reproduce with pen and ink.

Along the house on the street the men arranged a row of small earthen cooking stoves, which they had brought with them, each carrying two. The mode of carrying in this case, as well as in the transportation of any heavy load, is to use the shoulder as fulcrum and, laying on it an elastic wooden pole from whose ends hangs the burden, walk in steady balance, presenting the appearance of a pair of scales. Over the stoves were placed vessels of boiling water, over the vessels tubs with holes in the bottom and straw covers on top, in the vessels were heaps of rice washed perfectly white. The rice used in mochi-making is different from ordinary dinner rice; it is more glutinous when cooked and easily made into paste; it is a distinct variety selected in the beginning for the express purpose. The stoves are short hollow cylinders, open at the top and in the front; the top receives the bottom of the vessel, and the front opening or mouth ejects smoke and allows the feeding of fuel. They seemed on this occasion to blaze more brightly; we children went out and watched the dancing flames; they made our faces glow with their reflection.

When the rice was steamed long enough, it was transferred and made into paste in an utensil, like which I have seen nothing in this country. It is simply a stout trunk of a felled tree a few feet in height with its upper end scooped out. With it is a cylindrical block with a handle, a sort of pestle to press and strike upon the steamed rice. There was something joyous about the dull thumps when heard in the neighborhood, perhaps not to a foreign ear but to one brought up amongst customs associated with New Year holidays. And never at other times was our house so overflowing with hilarity as at this climax of domestic enjoyment. When the rice lost its granular appearance and became a uniform sticky mass, then it was placed upon a large board spread with rice flour. There it lay steaming, milk-white, this luxury of New Year,—luxurious even to the touch! The entire household flocked around it and made numerous round cakes. While our hands were busy, we interchanged many innocent jokes and merry laughs; the old people gave in to our sway, displaying a quiet humor in their looks.

We set up the New Year tree. It is a drooping willow tree thickly studded with rice-paste and hung with ornate cotton balls, painted cards, etc. Throughout the month of January it is to be seen in the parlor of every house nailed against the wall.

After nightfall on the last day of the old year a curious ceremony is performed. The worthy head of the family goes the round of his house with a box of hard burnt beans. Within every chamber he stands upright and throws a handful of the same, exclaiming at the top of his voice,—"Welcome Good Luck! Away with the Devil!" Now, the box used provisionally for a receptacle is a rice measure called măsu, which sounds like the verb meaning increase; and the beans are măme, which is the same as the noun meaning health, although written and accented differently. Putting them together we have a supplication in a play upon words,—"Increase health," or "May health increase!" Odd and fantastic as the notion appears, however, it is a hallowed custom and scrupulously observed. My father formerly performed the ceremony in our house; but when my eldest brother had grown up, he was assigned to the office, which he discharged with a comic gravity that I cannot forget.

The Japanese looks upon certain periods—I forget which—of his life as evil years. To avert hovering ill influences or to "drop" the years as they put it, the people take of the beans as many as their years, put them in paper bags together with a few pence and drop them at some cross-roads, taking care not to be seen. In this manner I have dropped several of my earlier bad years; I should have been wrecked a long time since, for life, but for the bags of beans!

In the same evening tradesmen desire to collect old bills and clear up the accounts of the passing year; and in order to do it they call at the houses of their debtors, lighting their way with lanterns which bear the signs of their commercial establishments. So general is this idea, and so customary has this proceeding become in time, that everybody expects it as a matter of course at the end of each year; debtors, too, are easily dunned. A consequence is one of the grandest displays of lanterns. What a delight it was to me to stand before my house and watch the countless lights move up and down the street! When I was older I was appointed lantern-bearer before the collector for my father, who instructed his man to give me points, incidentally, in business.

The next morning dawns, and the first day of the New Year is with us. Everybody seems happy, kind-hearted and filled with better feelings. Shopping housewives, grocers and hucksters of all sorts of holiday market goods have disappeared from the streets; the change is like that of Sunday morning from Saturday afternoon in an American city. All the houses are carefully swept and put in good order, and the people have on their best apparel. A kind of arch is erected in front of each dwelling. But it is not round, it is square. Two young pine trees are planted for the pillars, and cross-pieces of green bamboo are tied to them.

On this frame-work are placed the traditional simple ornaments; straw fringes, sea-weeds, ferns, a red lobster-shell, a lemon, dried persimmons, dried sardines and charcoal. These articles stand for many auspicious ideas; reflect a moment and they will come home clear to your mind. The pines, bamboos, sea-weeds and ferns are evergreens, fit emblems of constancy; the straw fringes are for excluding evil agencies—the lamb's blood on the door; the lobster by its bent form is indicative of old age or long life; the lemon is dăi-dăi—"generation after generation;" the dried persimmons are sweets long and well preserved; the sardines from their always swimming in a swarm denote the wish for a large family; and lastly, the stick of charcoal is an imperishable substance.

When the morning sun rises gloriously or snowflakes happen to fall (for we have snow in Japan), children leap out from under the arches, salute one another and begin to indulge in outdoor holiday games.

To speak about breakfast may be trespassing upon hospitality, but the Japanese New Year breakfast is something unique. The mochi makes up the main part. The unstuffed rice-cakes are cooked with various articles; potatoes, fish, turnips and everything palatable from land and sea is found with them. A person of ordinary capacity can scarcely take more than a few bowlfuls of the dish, but there are people brave enough to dispatch twenty or thirty at a time! For weeks after whenever idlers of the town come together there is always a warm discussion concerning their comparative merits in this respect. I have noticed that the good people of this republic also look upon Thanksgiving and Christmas as the days on which to indulge their best appetite; and I have heard persons telling the wonders of their stomachs and seeking opinions of the wise men around them, who are likewise dreaming over their pipes again of the turkeys, chicken-pies and plum-puddings that are gone by.

As the day advances, good towns-people in decorous antique garb appear in all directions, making New Year calls. Upon meeting their acquaintances they have not much to say, the chief thing being to keep the head going up and down with great formality,—a bow it is intended to be, yet a great deal more than that. It is almost an impossible act for one not trained so to do, unless he goes at it with the spirit of martyrdom. Of course, the parlor reception by ladies in white is something unheard of in the far East. Ladies are to be good and remain in the back parlor, except when their presence is desired by the gentlemen who do the honor of receiving; you often detect the bright eyes directed upon you through crannies.

The dinner is not so splendid an affair as the breakfast, but has many customary dishes to be served. The fact will strangely strike the reader, who associates in his mind such a sumptuous board as that of Christmas with the term dinner. In that figurative sense in which we frequently use it, it must properly be applied to the breakfast. I must mention here that in the New Year meals we put aside our crockery ware and take out from the store-room wooden bowls, japanned red inside and jet black outside with our family crest in gold. The children's are rendered more attractive with the pictures of flying cranes on the covers, and tortoises with wide-fringed tails among the waves on the exterior of the bowls, all in gold. A casual sight of them at other times, in my rummaging for things, was sufficient to awake in me a pleasant train of thoughts relative to the holidays. Oh, and that tremendous big fish, I must tell you about that! —Every family provides itself for New Year with a huge buri—Japanese name of course, I am ignorant of its proper zoological term; I obtained my first idea of the whale from this monstrous fish. It hangs in the kitchen from one of the rafters throughout the holidays; the cook cuts meat from it, and the family feasts upon it until it is reduced to a downright skeleton. My impression is that the fish is caught in some of the provinces bordering on the Pacific Ocean (Imabari looks on the inland sea) and sent to our town: certain it is, the article we procure is always salted. The rush for the buri in the market before New Year is just like the turkey bargaining before Thanksgiving in this country; the difference is that the buri is more expensive, and it is not everybody that can afford to buy one.

Taking advantage of the last evening's ceremony, in the course of the day female beggars appear in the mask of the Goddess Good Luck, and sing and dance for alms. That is tolerable. But a host more of strong male beggars, personating the devils with rattling bamboo bars and with hideously painted faces, plant themselves before the houses and demand in a strident authoritative voice a propitiation with hard coin. Some of them paint themselves with cheap red paint, representing the "red devils;" others smear themselves with the still more economical scrapings from the sides of the chimney, becoming thereby the "black devils." The idea of the devils of different colors came from the Buddhist's pictorial representation of Hell, wherein the demons are seen serving out punishment to the sinners,—throwing them into a sulphurous flame, a lake of blood, a huge boiling caldron and to dragon-snakes; giving them a free ride on a chariot of fire; driving them up a mountain beset with needles; pulling out the tongues of the liars; mashing the bodies as you do potatoes; and so forth. The pictures, by the bye, with many others of saints and martyrs, are the same in nature as the religious paintings of Rome and equally grand and magnificent. The bean ceremony, to conclude, although it might have banished imaginary devils, after all, has drawn together the very next morning an army of the flesh-and-blood devils that want to eat and drink.

## CHAPTER XI.

AMONG the recreations most fondly indulged in on the New Year holidays is kite-flying. This is so well known here that I have often been overwhelmed with questions regarding it by little Americans. Our kites are mostly rectangular, with heroes or monsters painted on them in most glaring colors. A wind instrument looking like a bow is sometimes fastened to the kite, and when the kite is in the air the wind strikes the string and makes a humming noise. At a kite-fight the combatants bring their flying kites in juxtaposition and strive to cut the string by friction. Now and then an unfortunate, hero or monster, is seen tossed about at the disposal of the wind, finding its fate upon the water, the tree-tops, or I know not where. At the height of kite-flying even those with more discretion enter into the full spirit of the young and build prodigious kites. I have actually seen one so large that, when flown high up on a fair windy day, the combined efforts of several men could scarcely hold it. It was a hard-fought tug-of-war; after much ado, with the aid of wrestlers and athletes, I remember, the monster was at length secured to the main front oaken pillar of a great building. The string fastened to such a kite is a strong twine hundreds of yards long, yet it often gives way. And to fly such a kite on the streets of a city is next to an impossibility; it will bump hard at houses and rake down the tiles (our houses are roofed with tiles) over the heads of passers-by; for which reason, it is always taken out to the open country and afterwards brought into town when it has gone well up in the air. What a mass of curious children surge beside the men who hold the kite by the string as they walk home!

I have sat many an afternoon after school whittling the bamboo frame for a modest kite. It was my most interesting employment; my father calls me into another room to run on an errand for him; I hear him plainly, but pretend otherwise and make him call repeatedly—ungrateful son! Upon hearing him approach and perceiving longer delay to be impossible, I break away from the agreeable occupation and emerge as cheerfully as I can, "Yes, sir, father." He inquires what I was about, reproves me for not answering him quickly and gives me to know that if I do not heed his behest he will surely throw my kite into the fire. After such interruptions, however, the important frame-work is done. Oh, what satisfaction I feel over it! Then I go to the kitchen and wheedle Osan into giving me a bit of boiled rice, which I make into paste on a piece of board with a bamboo spatula. With the paste I put white paper on the frame and leave it to dry. There are many little technical points in kite construction, but those I refrain from entering into in detail. When it is dry, I write on the kite confidentially with my own hand some appropriate word, say, Zephyr, in lieu of picture. I now tie the string and try its flight; it dashes at the eaves this way, pitches into the latticed windows that way, twirls in mid-air like a tumbler-pigeon, and in general behaves badly. Thereupon I take it down, add weight to the lighter side, attach a tail and do all to insure balance and equilibrium, and, then try it again.

Since coming to this country, the request has been put to me more than once by little friends that I should make them a genuine Japanese kite. But the want of tenacious paper and bamboo has always prevented me from complying with their wish.

As I write on, by the association of ideas I call to mind an event which greatly provoked me. I was fond of poking into and turning over old things up in the garret, as I hinted before, or I had archæological taste, to give it a dignified name. One day, much to my surprise, I came upon an old kite frame perhaps six feet by five, good for further use. I found it hidden behind a worm-eaten chest of drawers; it was constructed, I discovered, when my uncle was a boy; everybody in the house had forgotten all about it. I was instantly possessed with the desire to boast of a big kite, now that the frame was ready; and as if to help out my plan, some one recollected that the reel of string that went with the kite was put away in one of the drawers. This I immediately sought and found. These relics I guarded with great care until a visit from my uncle, who resided in the same town, when I produced them and got him to tell me about his kite. I could not have done a better thing; his old playthings before him put my uncle in mind of his boyhood; they created in him the wish to see them restored once more to their former usefulness; and he promised me he would attend to them himself.

Attend to them himself he did in a few days, taking as lively an interest as I did. Having papered the frame, we carried it to a man who painted show-bills. He painted on it a squatting Daruma in scarlet canonical robe, holding the high-priest's mace, a staff with a long tuft of white hair at one end, while the white untouched margin left by this large figure was stained blue. It was a glorious kite; the picture of Daruma, who was a great light of Buddhism, the founder of a new sect, who sat and thought through his whole life, suffering no disturbance from matters temporal—hence his *papier-mâché* image on a hemisphere of lead for the toy "tumbler;" Daruma, I started to say, looked out from our kite with a pair of immense goggle eyes, shaded by prominent shaggy eyebrows; a furrow ran down on either cheek from the side of his nose toward the corners of his mouth; large Hindoostanee ear-rings hung from the enlarged lobes of his ears; and I may here add that, notwithstanding his reputed sedentary habits, he is always drawn as a holy man of strong physical features.

So far, so good. My uncle, as might be anticipated, wanted to see how our kite would fly. Accordingly, we got a big boy to hold it up for us against the wind, and my uncle at a distance held the string ready to dash at a run. The signal was given, and away my uncle ran, and up rose the kite. Breathlessly I was watching. But it no sooner rose than it pitched sidewise and struck on the spikes upon the fences of the Mayor's house. I lost my heart! I did not cry just yet; the catastrophe was too big for utterance and too sudden; there was no time to weigh the calamity. The men pulled at the kite, which, I say, had stuck fast on the pointed black wooden bars bristling unmannerly in all possible directions. I bore the spikes an inveterate enmity ever after, till one day they were every one of them pulled down with the house, at which I felt extreme satisfaction. The tearing noise of the kite, however, rent my breast then; and the men, being persuaded at last of the futility of their proceeding, brought forward a ladder, and my uncle mounted it deliberately. I could not contain myself any longer; I ran into the house, threw myself on the floor and wept bitterly. After that I turned over the whole affair in my mind at leisure, lying on my back, studying the ceiling and sucking my finger in baby fashion. The phantom of the broken kite rose before me; I swallowed down my grief with difficulty. Who brought it about? Nobody else but uncle; yes, if uncle had not wished to try the kite it would not have happened. I whimpered afresh at the painful thought; I now reproached my uncle as much as I formerly thanked him. After a considerable lapse of time my uncle came in, crestfallen, with the tattered kite. But in dudgeon I would not speak to him or look at him; he very awkwardly endeavored to console me and with difficulty coaxed me to accept his atonement in patching the rents. The moisture of the glue, nevertheless, scattered the original colors and disfigured the beautiful picture. I forget how I forgave him that.

But to resume the holiday games. Boys play a sort of ball—the "pass and catch" part—with a good-sized dai-dai (lemon); we call it dai-dai rolling. We give each other the "grounder" repeatedly, so that even the hard-rinded Japanese fruit gets ruptured in a little time; then our business is to beat about for a supply of the new balls, which we invariably accomplish by knocking down the fruit from the unguarded arches. The people generally take the prank in good part.

Girls play out-of-doors with battledore and shuttlecock; they also play with cotton-balls, which they toss with their dainty hands against hard floors. They keep the ball bounding rhythmically between the palm of their hand and the floor, and hum songs in time with it.

At home and in the evening we play cards and other games. The favorite game of cards consists in giving out the first lines of couplets and endeavoring to pick out from the confusion of cards, in competition with others of the company, the particular cards on which are written the following lines; the one with the largest number of cards in the end is declared the winner. This game has the commendable feature of impressing on the mind celebrated poems; it is not merely time thrown away. Japanese poems, I remark in passing, are short and pithy; the classic "a Hundred Poems from a Hundred Poets" are characteristic and are consequently printed for the purpose of the game. The selected poems of the Tō dynasty, which in the annals of Chinese literature correspond to the English Elizabethan period, I mean in development and not in chronology, are substituted by scholars for the Japanese poems. We also play a kind of parchesi and a form of the game of authors, but whist, poker, casino, euchre, cribbage, etc., we know nothing of. Chess and checkers the Japanese are expert in, but they are not New Year games.

Fireside conversation, kind words and hearts constitute the quiet enjoyment and sunshine of the holidays. All things conspire to produce in us serene and tranquil pleasure, but nothing worth recording occurs in the remaining days. Some business-like briskness is manifested in the early hours of the second morning, for tradesmen observe the ancient custom of inaugurating the commerce of the opening year and give out presents to their customers.

Later in the spring—I forget the exact date—all the straw ornaments, withering wreaths and the like used in the decoration are brought together and burnt up with religious care on a broad sandy river flat just beyond the town. The day appointed for the rite is another gala-day of the calendar, at least in Imabari. For some time previous to the occasion, the straw relics of all the houses of a street are carefully collected in one spot, and then such as are artists exercise ingenuity to produce some recognizable shape out of the heap that may catch the eye of spectators, on its way to the place of combustion. Street vies with street in originality in fashioning the straw stack and takes care not to divulge what it is constructing until the day of display, then it ostentatiously raises the finished work, whatever it may be, on a high movable platform or pedestal on wheels, which takes its position in the line of march with those of the other streets. The whole town is curious to know what is in the parade and rushes out to behold.

I recall only one among many things which my own street produced on such occasions; it was a military cap and a trumpet joined together. Innumerable sheets of gilt paper were wasted in giving the monstrous form of a trumpet the appearance of bright, shining brass; the cap, too, was wonderfully like the real imported thing. These barbarian outlandish articles, having been adopted by the Japanese government at the time, were exciting the attention and comments of the people; hence, the striking reproduction of them on a greatly magnified scale made everybody utter a little cry of surprise and admiration. I forget to which of us the inspiration came.

The pedestal or platform has two large massive iron rings in front, to which are tied stout ropes; the younger part of the inhabitants of the street hang together in two rows and haul the decorated burden. Song and chorus, and the heavy wheels creak onward a short distance, then stop: song again and chorus; then another pause.

Among the crowd we occasionally meet a man carrying a bamboo stick, one end of which is split and holds half-a-dozen hardened mochis. He intends to scorch the cakes in the flames of the relics and, upon returning home, to divide them among his family and eat them for the miraculous power they are then believed to possess.

This is, in short, the manner in which we observe and end our great national holiday of New Year. Of late, it is to be regretted, many of the old customs are omitted by the people who have got modern notions into their heads. Innovations of the latter days not very desirable or in good taste are fast gaining ground. A few years more, and, I fear, the neglect of time-honored observances will be complete in Japan.

## CHAPTER XII.

We have a great many other holidays; it is impossible to speak of them all. Simply to name some, there are God Fox's day on the second of the second month; the Feast of Dolls, for little girls, on the third of the third month; the Feast of Flags for little boys on the fifth of the fifth month; the ablution mass in the sixth month; the Tanabata (eve of the seventh) on the seventh of the seventh month; the day of chrysanthemum flowers and the festival of Inoko late in the fall, not to mention festivals of several local deities. The vital importance of these holidays to us children centered in the dainties and delicacies with which our mothers and sisters served us then and not often at ordinary times. We enjoy boiled red beans and rice on the second of February; rice-flour cakes wrapped in the leaves of a species of oak called kashiwa on the fifth of May; rice-flour cakes daubed with the an on the day of the Buddhistic ceremony of ablution; roast and boiled chestnuts and rice and chestnuts on the ninth of September; and the saké on almost all occasions, but with a spray of peach blossom inserted in the bottle on the third of March, and a bunch of chrysanthemum flowers on the chrysanthemum day.

In Tanabata and Inoko the boys of the town used to club together on payment of a small fee, the biggest among them presiding over their affairs by common consent. Our first work is to canvass such houses in consecutive order as have large front rooms, soliciting their owners to loan us the room for a few days for a temporary club-house, free of charge. And when we are given by a generous man the use of his house, thither we convey our common property. The property comprises the scroll gods, a holy mirror, the golden gohĕi (a sacred brass ornament), a pair of pewter saké bottles, splendid curtains, a large number of the sambo (offering stand of white wood, sometimes varnished), countless Japanese lanterns, timber and board ready to be put together for an altar looking like a staircase, Chinese crimson felt carpets, several drums and certain kinds of bells. These things have been handed down to us by successive generations of boys, repaired each year and additions made by donations or by "chipping in," and all nicely packed in chests, on the sides and covers of which we read the names of some that have died, and of others that are yet living though well-nigh to the grave. The boys take good care of the old heirlooms, that they may transmit them without injury to their successors. The older boys take the things out and set up a place of worship; on the days of festivity the members come to the headquarters with their lunch-boxes well stocked. We assemble not to worship really, you might as well understand now, but to have a good time. Fruits and cakes have been taken in by the managers from the wholesale merchants, and are piled up in pyramids on the samboes upon the steps of the altar; they are to be divided equally among the stockholders afterwards. The lanterns are lighted brilliantly at night; a special lantern is hoisted on a very high pole planted before the house to signify our quarters.

At Tanabata we march through the streets with green bamboo trees, rending the air with certain shouts and beating the instruments, and upon meeting the boys of other streets have a scuffle. The scene is a confusion of bamboos and bits of rainbow-colored papers which are tied plentifully to the branches. After a hot contest we come home to the club, eat a hearty lunch and celebrate the incidents of our victory. The day after the festival we take our bamboos to the sea and cast them off to be drifted away by the waves and finally up to the Heavenly Stream or the Milky Way, where the gods may read our wishes written on the rainbow-colored papers. On this day everybody goes swimming, because the sea-monkey is handcuffed that can lengthen one arm enormously at the expense of the other, and draws in and drowns people, especially boys who go swimming in opposition to their mothers' remonstrance.

At Inoko we bring forth our gorin. A gorin is a spherical stone, usually granite, with an iron belt loose in a groove around the great circumference; the belt has many small rings through it. A club of boys possesses five to ten gorins of various sizes. To the rings are attached ropes, and calling at the families to which came male offspring during the year, the boys utter words of blessing and pound the ground by pulling up and down the solid stone. After a series of thumps a depression is left behind. We hold gorin collisions with neighboring powers. A challenge is sent to other clubs to meet us with their best gorin on neutral ground at such a time, that we may know which is stronger. The war gorin is equipped for the contest with a network of ropes, exposing a portion of the surface that shall deal the blow; the leading boys guide it in the battle by several strong ropes. Generally in the collision more noise is heard than the clash; however, not rarely the contest is kept up until one or the other splits through the core, and the opposition is so strong as to cause older people to interfere in the affair, because it infallibly entails unpleasant feeling between the parties and a scrimmage at all times. I call to mind that our club used to plume itself upon the strength and durability of its gorins; no, not one received so much as a crack, albeit many and severe were the tests to which they had been subjected.

Besides the gorin sports, at Inoko we get up wrestling matches. On the yard of the club-house we build a circular bank of clay and fill the inside with sand; in this all the members contend in practice. Small as I was, I did not like to be thought out of fashion, and to pay for my uncalled-for prowess suffered from sores and bruises. In a body we visit the headquarters of the other clubs and negotiate the matches, which take place immediately on the spot in full view of both parties.

The ceremony of ablution is chiefly observed by Shinto priests. (Shinto is the native faith, holding up the sun for the center figure of worship and eight millions of spirits besides.) The way they observe it in my province consists in setting up in the temple-yard three large hoops of the sasaki tree (sacred to Shintoism) and inviting the people to pass through them. The hoops are supposed to take up the people's sins and transgressions, leaving them clean and fit for the further grace of the gods. Thus loaded with the earthly corruptions and loathsome pollutions of man, the round bands of the fresh, green trees, thickly stuck with zigzag white paper hangings, at the end of the day are taken to running water and washed thoroughly or more commonly committed to the sea.

At about the same time Buddhist priests hold mass for dead sinners. The different sects have different notions. My family were formerly parishioners to a temple of the Hokké sect; therefore, I best remember the mass as observed by that particular denomination. The church society and its officers meet in the vestry to take action in the preparation of floating lanterns. These are hasty, rude contrivances which the active of the parishioners volunteer in getting up; it does not require much skill in carpentry to make them, but it takes time to make so many. Look at one: an odd piece of board for the bottom, two split bamboos bent and stuck on it like the handle of a basket one across the other, and a hood of paper glued round the whole; a nail in the center holds a penny candle. All very inartistic indeed, as befits their use, as we shall see presently.

On the mass day all about the temple are strung up an untold number of the lanterns. Now, devout old folks and young come in streams all day to put up prayers for their beloved dead, and those so inclined buy the lanterns for the purpose of lighting the way for the departed. The goods when paid for are handed over by the presiding elders, who have charge of the sale, to the priest and assistant priests; they write sûtra verses on them and order them to be left before the altar. If business is good, by the latter part of the evening the entire stock is disposed of; the till rattles with money, and the priests are in good cheer. Then follows a great chanting and beating of drums, and after prayers have been said once for all, the lanterns are put on board several boats and the drums and cymbals also carried to enliven the next scene; the priests and committee walk down to the shore slowly. Things being placed aright, out they pull on the heaving sea—the incoming tide having been looked to beforehand, so that at high tide the lighted lanterns may be set afloat and go drifting at their will with the falling flood.

Ah, they are gone, the skiffs! We discern them no more. I want you to understand that it is a dark night, otherwise my picture isn't so good, although in point of fact the moon does often chance to look up on the occasion. And the moonlight on the swelling tide is not very bad, I acknowledge, yet, you see, I wish to preserve the grand effect of "fire and darkness." So, pray, gentle reader, indulge my fancy this time; I won't always ask this. Well, it's a dark night then: as the boats slip out of our sight we can hear the lapping noise that comes of their swaying from side to side caused by the queer Japanese mode of sculling. Ere long we cease to hear it; the vessels are well out in the obscurity. Do we not see anything of them? Not quite. The lights they convey show us their whereabouts. We are all this while on shore, mind you. The onset of water seems to take uncommon delight in driving us up, chuckling to itself along the beach, until at last we are crowded into a narrow strip of sand with the rest of the spectators. There! it's up to the high-water-mark; we won't be annoyed any longer. Let's sit down.

While we watch, ten thousand points of light dot the expanse; no finer illumination, I for one, ever expect to see on earth; and soon there blazes out a great ruddy flame from the chief priest's boat, amid the confused echoes of prayers on all the vessels. That is the end of it, friends; sit still and look on, if you choose,—many indeed do so—and observe the lights recede and drift away, or die out. Of these some never return and are believed to have gone where they were bidden, others and a majority, to be frank with you, are washed ashore next morning shattered into fragments.

## CHAPTER XIII.

It is wonderful how the memory brings up, as I write, ten thousand irrelevant trivialities,—delightful to me, nevertheless,—many of which have no claim to be placed here, except that they are more or less related to the temple. Verily, the faculty of memory is a godsent gift, a boon of solitary hours.

Our temple was the nearest to the sea of the row on Temple street, which I referred to in the earlier portion of this sketch. The head-priest was an amiable, gentle person, very learned they say, though giving no indication of being such. He did his duty, to be sure, in sermons, but never cared much to distinguish himself in eloquence; he would rather read or entertain visitors in the quiet of his tastefully upholstered zashiki (guest room), sipping the excellent Uji tea and viewing the artistic beds of chrysanthemum laid out with great formality. He cultivated exquisite flowers; the slender stems bent under the large flaunting heads, and the priest-gardener took pity and provided them with firm props; he was as attached to them as a father to his children. If a storm by night passed over them and he discovered them in the morning sagged, matted, and drenched with rain, his compassion knew no bounds.

It must be confessed that at times his fine taste shaded into squeamishness; he could not help being captious about his servitor's slipshod management of business, and yet extremely averse was he to giving his own opinion utterance, always turning aside in silent disgust. He suffered little children, however, nay, loved them; he took quite a fancy to me, calling me pet names, gladdening me on my visits with goodies and a bunch of chrysanthemum flowers from his garden, and always sending me home safely by a boy-priest. This last, found vegetating in almost every temple, is a young lad of poor parentage sent thither to be taken care of out of charity. The specimen I found here was a poor boy, hence happy; he was sure of dinner now and more full of fun than well became his cloth.

Once he frightened me half to death. It happened in this way: I accompanied some one of my relatives to our family burying ground in the temple yard, on the eve of the annual memorial day for the dead, when every family sends a delegate to the tombs and invites the spirits home. The delegate delivers the oral message with profound respect and formality, bowing low to the ground before the ancestral tombstones as in an august presence. Then he turns about and asks the invisible to get on his back, secures him with both hands behind and gravely walks homeward. At home, in the yard on a bed of sand taken from the sea-shore a fire is built of flax stems, according to religious custom. This is called the "reception fire." The spirits are next requested to alight carefully at the high home altar so as not to bruise their shanks. In Japan each house has a sacred closet wherein are enshrined images, ancestral tablets, charms and amulets, where cake and oranges, flowers and incense are offered, and before which the family commemorate the days of their ancestors' death. This elevated place is called the "Buddha's shelf." Let me remark here that the Eastern people are regardful of their dead; they do not slight them because they are dead. Revile as you may and wrongly call it "ancestor worship," the spirit that prompts the act is entirely praiseworthy. Besides the closet, the tops of cabinet, cupboard and similar pieces of household furniture are turned into the depositories of Shinto relics and paper gods. These "gods' shelves" are, too, carefully served with such offerings as salt fish, saké, and light in the evening.

But I am wandering from the main narrative; my talk too often gallops into minor tracks unbridled. As I commenced the narration, I was stooping before the resting places of my grandfather (of whose quiet departure from our hearth, by the bye, I haven't told you), of my grandmother and of my sister who passed on before I had ever thought of appearing. Regarding the last two relatives of mine, having never seen them in life, I was in the habit of asking a heap of questions in the tiresome inquisitiveness of children. My mother deigned to tell me, especially in a reminiscent mood, a great deal concerning them, without minding my sisters, who took occasion to upbraid me merrily on this, my singular ignorance, in face of my other positive assertion that I had witnessed my mother's wedding. Dear mamma's stories, interesting as they are, touching as they do not a little on the pleasures, fashions and general social regimé of Old Japan, I feel obliged to omit. For the present, I must go on with my own story.

I was stooping, I say, before the tombs, all about being silent and gloomy; my young animated imagination dwelling not on my grandfather's goodness but on old wives' awful tales of graveyards and dark nights, pale apparitions and grinning skeletons; and my whole being surcharged with fear, requiring but the shrill wind to make my hair stand on end, and ready to start at my own shadow, when suddenly there came a moan from behind the adjoining slabs, and a moment later a ghost shot up with a wild shriek. I drew back involuntarily and caught my breath, so did my companion. Then the ghost shook its gaunt sides and burst out laughing in ghoulish delight. We were taken aback, but soon rallied courage sufficiently to peer at the merry spook. How provoking! The young priest stood on one of the tombstones, with the broad sleeve of his monkish habiliment over his face. He came down to us quickly, wearing a mischievous smile, passed over the whole thing as a huge jest, putting in a slight excuse for causing our undue alarm, and politely offered his service in carrying the flowers and water-pail. His words and manners smoothed away our ruffled temper and rendered a scolding impossible; a few more hours made it look too slight to report to the head-priest. In the main the young priest had the best of us; he earned what he liked better than a good dinner,—some capital fun.

And in this connection, here comes bounding toward me in my remembrance our pet dog Gem. I will relate how he came to be so closely associated in my thought with the grave;.it is a sad, good story. My young brother, who had a boy's fondness for animal pets in an eminent degree, got him from another boy whose dog had a litter of several puppies. When my brother brought him home in his arms, Gem was but a mass of tender flesh covered over with soft down; he had just been weaned; consequently by night he yelped, and cried piteously for his mother, under the piazza where my brother shielded him from the paternal eye. My father was not a great lover of pets: the cat he could not bear for her soft-voiced, velvet-pawed deceitfulness; the dog for his belligerent, deep-mouthed barks at strangers and for fear of his becoming mad in summer time; and the canary bird—poor thing —it was too bad that people should deprive it of its native freedom.

We had our doubts, therefore, how Gem and papa were to get along. However, we were not without a ray of hope that in time they would come to be good friends, for papa had once shown that he did not altogether lack the love of dumb animals. It was when I began to love the little white and spotted mice penned in a box with a glass front and a wheel within. My father suffered them to be kept in the house out of his love for me; gradually his curiosity was awakened to take a look occasionally at what his son exhibited such absorbing interest in; next he became a keen admirer of my little revelers,—their gambols, their assiduous turning of the wheel, their cunning way of holding rice grains, and their house-keeping in a wad of cotton in the drawer beneath, to which they could descend by a hole in the floor of the box. After a while I grew negligent about them, and then it was my father who fed them and took care of them.

On the whole, he bade fair to come to a better understanding with our precious Gem. Nevertheless, Gem—or rather my young brother—had trouble with him during his canine minority. When the puppy had grown big, true to our prophecy, my father began to show his just appreciation of him. Gem would sit beside him on his hind legs at meal times and watch intently the movements of the chopsticks, with his head inclined on one side one moment and on the other the next, letting out an occasional faint guttural cooing by way of imploring a morsel. Should there haply fall from the table an unexpected gift, say a sardine's head, Gem with the utmost alacrity would pick it up and occupy himself for a few minutes, then, licking his chops and wagging his tail, he would turn up to my father a gaze at once thankful for what was given and hopeful for more. Little Gem took a fancy to grandpa, and when the children were away at school, he would pay him a visit and pitpat into his room unceremoniously, like one of the grandchildren, when the old gentleman was dozing over the past at the kotatsu (fire-place). This Gem of ours had an idea that it was rude to surprise one in his meditation, and thought it proper to stop short a few yards from grandpa and utter one of his gutturals, as much as to say, "How do you do, grandpa?" Whereat our good, old grandpa was obliged to break off to receive his fourfooted visitor cordially.

A time came when grandpa was no more, and a perfect stillness settled on our home. Dear little Gem could ill comprehend what all the house meant and went about as happily and innocently as before: he had now his playmates all day at home. His conduct caused us to think how glad we should be to know no grief, and to such a place we felt sure must our grandpa have gone. Early every morning for the first week or two somebody from the house repaired to the church-yard to see that things were right and to put up prayers; once or twice Gem was taken along for company, and since then he counted it his duty to attend us to the temple. My father and I would get up some morning on this errand, and no sooner had we appeared at the gate than Gem uncurled from his comfortable sleeping posture, rose and shook his hair and looked his "I am ready." He generally paced before us, but frequently tarried behind to salute his dog-neighbor with a good morning. Sometimes he would course sportively away from our sight; we whistled loud without any response; but knowing he could find his way back, we gave up the search and hastened to the temple. Upon our arrival, before grandpa's stone sat a little dog looking out on the alert. Gem received us in the capacity of host and conducted us to the grave, saying as plainly as ever dog said, "Don't you see? I know the way."

One morning we rose to find our Gem gone. Inquiries revealed him lying at a short distance from the gate, with his fur dyed in his own life-blood. He was dead! Whether a prowling, ferocious animal had fallen on him in the night, or a cruel human brute had inflicted the wounds without just cause, we could not ascertain. My young brother took Gem's cruel death to heart; my father, too, felt deeply the sad fate of the now-to-him priceless pet. And here naturally ends the story of our dog.

In our temple, as well as in those of all other denominations, the birthday of the great common teacher Shaka (Gautama) is observed. It falls on the eighth, I think, of April; the observance is simple and quiet except for the distribution of ubuyu. In the East, when a child is born the midwife immediately plunges it in a tub of warm water. This water is called ubuyu or first bath. On the eighth of April, in every temple a bronze basin is placed before the altar; in the center of the basin stands a bronze image of the Infant Shaka; his attitude is much like that of the Boy Christ pictured in the illustrated Bibles and the Sunday-school cards as teaching a group of the scribes. The myth relates a marvelous account of his rising upright in the bath-tub and telling his astonished parents and old midwife whence he came, pointing to heaven, and what his mission on earth was. His exact words are recorded in the Buddhist's scriptures.

The bronze vessel is filled with a decoction of a certain dried herb whose taste resembles liquorice. The drink is popularly known as the "sweet tea." The worshiper pours the liquid over the idol with a small dipper and then sips a little of the same, numbling some devotional words.

The excitement of the day consists in the children's running to the temples, during the early part of the morning, with bottles for the sweet tea or the ubuyu, as it is called in this instance. In the temple kitchen the cook has boiled gallons and gallons of it, and from the dawn that functionary is prepared for the hubbub and the hard task of dispensing it expeditiously to the throng. As the holiday comes in the same season of the year as Easter, the floral decoration of the temples are beautiful; the bronze roof above the basin and image is always artistically covered over with a quantity of a native flower named gengé, which the botanist may classify under the genus *Trifolium*, if I may trust my early observation. The flowers literally color the fields pink in the spring.

## CHAPTER XIV.

In describing a distant view of Imabari I made mention of a sea-god's shrine jutting out into the sea: the festival of that god as well as of one situated on the harbor and of another on the bank of a river takes place in the summer. The people go worshiping in the evening. A myriad of lights twinkle in the air and are reflected on the water below; refreshment stands line the approaches to the shrine, and their vociferous proprietors assert their articles to be the very best; the crackers go off like pop-corn and scintillating fireworks dart upward now here, now there and everywhere, ending in resplendent showers of sparks; drums are beating incessantly; the people jostle each other in getting on and off the steps of the shrine; along the beach are seated a multitude cooling in the breeze, the children amusing themselves by digging pits in the sand and making ducks and drakes upon the water. These are the salient features of the midsummer nights' festivities. The last but not the least attraction is the reviving breeze along the shore; the worshipers generally go through the offering of pennies, clapping of hands, bowing and murmuring of prescribed, short prayers as hastily as practicable, that they may have more time on the beach.

On the fifteenth of August a great festival takes place every year in my native town. It is in honor of a patron deity. Everybody is up with the dawn, children especially are up ever so early in the morning. Paper lanterns hoisted high in the air on long bamboo sticks are moving toward the shrine. It is yet dark, but the people forget sleepiness in the bracing air of the daybreak and in the expected joy. Every store is cleared of its merchandise and has a temporary home-shrine erected, the god being a scroll with the deity's name written on it. Two earthen bottles of saké are invariably offered.

When the day is fully come, the procession starts from the permanent abode of the gods. A huge drum comes foremost, then a number of men in red masks with peaked noses, representing fabulous servants of the gods. Then come two portable shrines built like a sedan chair, and the rear is brought up by yagura-daiko. This last is a large frame-work of varnished wood carried by men. On the top of it a large bass-drum is placed, and with four boys around it. The boys are dressed in fancy costumes and beat time for the songs of the men below. The men are all dressed in white and seem at first to keep the presence of their gods in mind; but soon they get drunk, being treated with wine in every house, and spatter their garments with mud.

As the shrines pass, the men get into the houses, seize the earthen bottles of saké and pour the contents over them. These men also get tipsy and treat the beautiful shrines rudely, turning them wildly and throwing them hard on the ground; so that, at the end of the day, there is nothing left of them but their trunks. This rude usage became an established custom, and the portable shrines are built very strong.

A few days previous to the festival, boys prepare for it by constructing jumonji. Two slender elastic timbers are tied together in the form of a cross; one boy mounts it, and his comrades lift him up by applying their shoulders to the four ends. They march up and down the streets, singing festal songs, and challenge boys of other streets to come forth and have a "rush."

Not far from my native town there stands a high peak called Stone-hammer. It is customary for older boys to scale the lofty mountain and pay tribute to the deity on the top of it. They get somebody who has been there before for their leader. The preparation for the holy hazardous journey is rigorous. They bathe in cold water for months previously, live on plain diet, and pass the time in prayers and penances. Were their hearts and bodies unclean, it is reported that, on their ascent to the shrine, the gods' messengers—creatures half man, half eagle—would grasp them by the hair and fly away among the clouds and often kill them by letting them fall upon the crags and down into the valleys.

When a set of the hardy youths start out for the venturesome pilgrimage, they are dressed in white cotton clothes, shod with straw sandals, and have their long hair thoroughly washed and hanging loose. Each carries a pole with a tablet nailed on one end, on which is written the name of the mountain god. They shout a short prayer in unison, blowing a horn at intervals. My elder brother who went with one of these bands told me that the journey is very toilsome and dangerous. There are three chains to help in climbing three perpendicular heights. At times he was above the clouds, heard the peals of thunder beneath his feet and felt extremely cold. The leader sometimes holds a wayward youth on the verge of a precipice by way of discipline and demands whether he will reform or whether his body shall be cast into the gorge below.

The pilgrims bring home for souvenirs the leaves and branches of sacred trees and distribute them among their friends and relatives. The friends and relatives, for their part, wait for them at the outskirts of the town. At an appointed hour the spreads are awaiting the weary worshipers. Little brothers and sisters strain their ears to catch the faintest echoes of the horns and shouts. When the youthful travelers are back and fully established again in their homes, marvelous are the stories that they deal out to their friends.

I have been consuming a good deal of time and space in describing amusements and holidays; it is high time to revert to studies. I had been going to school all this time. The spirit of rivalry at school was fostered to such an extent that we felt obliged to go to the teachers in the evenings for private instruction. The teacher sits with a small, low table before and an andon beside him. The andon is the native lamp, cylindrical in shape, perhaps five feet in height and a foot in diameter; the frame is made of light wood, and rice-paper is pasted round it. In the inside is suspended a brass saucer, sometimes swinging from a cross-piece at the top and sometimes resting on a cross-bar in the middle; the vessel holds the rush-wick and vegetable oil extracted from the seed of a *Crucifer*. The andon gives but feeble light and is now entirely displaced by the kerosene lamp. In lighting a lamp, prior to the importation of matches, we struck sparks with flint and steel on a material inflammable as gun cotton, called nikusa, and from it secured light with sulphur-tipped shavings called tsukegi (lighting-chips).

Close to the andon the pupils, one at a time, in the order of their arrival, bring their books and sit *vis-a-vis* with the teacher. The latter first hears the pupil read the last lesson and then, after it has been thoroughly reviewed, reads for him the next lesson. He does it looking at the pupil's book from the top; the learner follows him aloud, pointing out every word he reads with a stick. This is repeated until the scholar has nearly learned the text. The scholar then returns home to go over the lesson by himself. In this manner I have torn my Japanese and Chinese authors, just as an American boy blots his Cæsar and Virgil; and certain passages come up even now as spontaneously as the translation of "*Gallia est omnis divisa in partes tres.*"

In school an examination was held at the end of each month; how hard we used to work for it! It decided one's standing in class, and all through the following month he had to remain in a given seat. Everybody wished to be at the head and that bred strong emulation. The night before the examination I would study and read aloud all the evening; as it became late my eyelids tended to droop and my voice to falter; my father would bid me not to be over-anxious and retire. The next morning he would wake me early in compliance with my request, and light me a lamp to study by. It was a bad habit, I grant; but if I work half as conscientiously now as I did then I shall be the wiser for it.

My class was composed of about six members; we met in each other's houses outside of school hours to go over our reviews together. One of the boys was a carpenter's son and possessed with a mechanical craze. Whenever we gathered in his house he would offer, unsolicited, to explain and exhibit a gimcrack he had made with his father's tools, and we did scarcely any studying. Another of our schoolmates was a farmer's son, a big shame-faced lad sent to our beloved master's to be educated in the city; he boarded with him. Country-fellow as we called him, he acquired his preceptor's hand in writing so well that nobody in school chose to pick a quarrel with him on the question of brush handling. But no mortal man is without a peccadillo—our boy was always observed to be moving his jaws and chewing more candies than were good for him. The third was a staid druggist's son, sedate as his father and as particular in trifling matters; he was "awfully smart," as the phrase is, in his studies, having pursued them conscientiously; and besides, he belonged as a matter of course to the category of "good boys." I used to sleep with him in his house sometimes and study arithmetic with him.

Here parenthetically I must describe the Japanese bed. It is a very simple affair: a thick quilt is taken out of a closet and spread directly on the floor; you lie down on it and pull another quilt over yourself, and you have the bed. There is no bedstead; therefore, fleas have a picnic at your expense if the room is not well swept. In the morning you fold the quilts and put them back in the closet, and space is given for the day. Our pillow is no comfort to a weary head, it being simply a hard block of wood; often it is a box with a drawer at the end. The use of this kind of pillow or support was formerly imperative for the men and is still to the women for the protection of the head-dress from ruin and the bedclothes from the bandoline. The sterner sex of our population now-a-days crop their hair after the fashion of their European brothers, and have in great part given up the wooden block for a soft pillow.

My schooling was continued for some time with satisfactory results, and I advanced grade after grade well-nigh to the end of the common school instruction, when my father saw fit to remove me and put me in a store so that I could be a credit to myself as a business-man's son. I was an apprentice in two trades at different times and yet unsettled in mind and anxious to go back to school. I might go on telling all about the period of my apprenticeship, and things I learned and people I observed during that time; how I finally carried the day and returned to my studies; how I studied Chinese and how I struck out in English; how I went to Kioto and struggled through five years' academic training; and how a few years ago I borrowed money and sailed for America. But that would be writing a real autobiography, which would be disagreeable to me as well as distasteful to the reader. In the story told so far I ought to have, perhaps, prudently suppressed everything personal and brought forward only those experiences that the generality of Japanese boys are destined to undergo. Neither have I exhausted by any means the incidents of my own childhood; at this moment I am conscious of things of more importance than those set down on the foregoing pages welling up in the fountain of memory. But I have written enough to try the patience of my indulgent reader, and I myself have grown weary of my own performance; it is therefore excusable, I hope, to draw this narrative abruptly to an

**END.**

www.ingramcontent.com/pod-product-compliance
Lightning Source LLC
Chambersburg PA
CBHW022137160426
43197CB00009B/1326